Letters Home

From Civil War Soldier

Charles Gamble

1862-1864

I0172556

Compiled by

Mark Flinchpaugh

Second Edition: December 20, 2011

ISBN
978-0-615-49094-6

Published by J L Flinchpaugh Publishing Company
St. Joseph, Missouri 64503

Introduction

The letters you are about to read were written in the 1860's by Charles W. Gamble to his wife and family back home in Salem County, New Jersey. Charles was a soldier serving on the Union side in the Civil War with the 12th Regiment, New Jersey Volunteers, Company D.

Years ago, my family and I were in the furniture and antiques business and sometimes purchased whole estates. Nearly forgotten for many years were these old letters I had set aside. These letters were so historical and fascinating; I felt I just had to publish them to share with everyone. They were copied to this book as close to the original as possible, including misspelled words. For clarity I have taken the liberty to separate each letter of correspondence into more readable paragraphs without altering the actual wording.

This book is much more than just a detached historian's view of Civil War events. It is a fascinating and personal account of a common soldier's life serving his country and fighting to keep the Union intact. Told from the intimate perspective of a typical volunteer soldier, you will glean interesting tidbits of historical information not usually found in books about the Civil War.

You will come to feel that you know Charles personally as you read his actual letters about his daily activities during the war. From mundane chores to the horrors of battle at Gettysburg, you will experience Civil War life through Charles' own words.

A carpenter by trade, Charles Gamble was 34 years old when he answered his country's call for duty. Leaving behind his beloved wife Eliza, his baby boy George, and other family members, he voluntarily joined the Union army in August of 1862 to, as he stated, "preserve the country and the constitution." Several times in his letters he frankly wrote that he might not come back home alive, but that he was serving for a just cause.

As Charles was nobly serving his country to save what his forefathers had accomplished, the hardships became increasingly difficult. The living conditions were frequently deplorable-- not enough food, contaminated drinking water, heavy packs while marching through the mud soaked countryside and trying to stay warm during the bitterly cold weather. And of course there was always the imminent threat of engaging the enemy-- the Rebels. The pain and suffering was ever present and death and destruction was common but Charles courageously pressed on for the good of the country.

History comes alive in these sometimes horrific but always insightful, loving letters sent home almost 150 years ago by Charles W. Gamble.

Mark Flinchpaugh

Letter Excerpts
Contents

v

Dear Father Mother and Wife; Washington, December 11, '62
*"Our Captain says that we have to go to Virginia or a place about
65 miles from here; and he says that he thinks that we will have to
march all the way there if they don't get a steamer to take us"....*

Dear Parents and Wife; - Virginia-December 20, 1862 *"The mud
on the road was about six inches deep and we had to ford runs
about 12 inches deep. When we would stop to rest our boys would
lighten their knapsacks by throwing out pants, drawers, shirts, and
trowsers and some even threw away their blankets and some their
whole knapsacks"*

Dear Parents and Wife; - Falmouth, Virginia. January 10, 1863.
*"I have been down to the Falmouth since I wrote you my last letter
and saw the place and a hard looking place it is too. It looks as if it
had seen some very rough times; some of the brick houses with all
of the wood work burnt out and nothing standing but the walls and
no fences to be seen anywhere"*

Dear Brother and Sister; - Camp Near Falmouth, Virginia.
January 12th, 1863 *"We see some rough times here once in a while
and some nice times too; but when we go over to the 24th regiment
and others that have been in battle we come back to our own and
are well contented with our own faire"*

Dear Parents and Wife; - Falmouth, Virginia January 20th, 1863
*"They have detailed me out for a cook and I am now exempt from
all duty as long as I am cook."... "Our orders have just been read
to us that we have got to cross the Rappahannock and to clean our
guns and get ready for a fight with the enemy"*

Dear Brother and Sister; - Falmouth, Virginia. February 2nd, 1863
*"I have about 70 to cook for and it keeps me busy all the time; I
have been at it about 2 weeks and I believe it agrees with me better
than to do my duties as a soldier as I am excused from duty while
I am a cook"*

Dear Parents and Wife; Falmouth, Virginia.   February 3rd, 1863.
*"We don't know but what we may stay here all winter now as
Burnside has left us and the army now is quiet. Hooker has now*

Dear Parents and Wife;-Gainesville,Vir., June 25th, 1863 *"there I saw a sad sight, one that I never had seen before; it was dead soldiers buried or undertaken to be, but they had only had dirt thrown over them, and some of their hands and arms were sticking out with the flesh all off of them; and some with their heads sticking out, some with one leg and foot with a shoe on. I tell you it was a sad sight for me to look at and a hard one to think of"*................67

Dear Brother and Sister;- Camp near Culpepper, Virginia. October 1st, 1863. *"I would like to see you with your little one in your lap and see if you look motherly and if I should live to get home I will come down and see you"*

Dear Brother and Sister; - Camp near Culpepper, Virginia October 2nd, 1863. *"We are in a piece of large timber and the squirrels are very thick here; I have seen as high as 6 on one tree and I have seen 2 flocks of wild turkeys since I have been here. I saw them and that was all for they were out of my sight as quick as a flash we are not allowed to shoot or I would have had some squirrel soup and a turkey dinner before this time"*

Dear Eliza;- Camp near Culpepper, Virginia. October 5th, 1863 *"We received our pay again last Saturday and after taking out my clothes bill I only had $3.94 coming to me, so I cannot send you any money this time but I will next time."*

Dear Parents and Wife;- On the Bull Run Battlefield October 17th, 1863. *"I have caught a very heavy cold, and having the rheumatism in my back, makes me feel very bad and one time I thought I would have to fall out, but my ambition was great enough to let me continue on the march."*

Dear Parents and Wife;- Camp on the Warrenton Branch R.R. In sight of the Town of Warren, Va. October 24th, 1863. *"We have been in three battles since we have been on the march, and one very sharp one, but we drove them every time."*

Dear Parents and Wife; - Milton, Virginia November 12th, 1863. *"I think I fell away 20 lbs. in two weeks; the captain says if I keep on falling away there will be nothing of me in a little while"*

PREFACE

The year was 1862. The terrible "War Between The States"----now known as the Civil War----was still dragging on after nearly 15 months of fighting. President Abraham Lincoln was greatly concerned that the Confederacy was making headway, so he issued a request for 300,000 new Union volunteers.

President Abraham Lincoln
February 12, 1809 – April 15, 1865
16th President of the United States

In New Jersey for example, citizens walking the streets and roads of Gloucester, Cumberland, and Salem counties might have encountered this recruiting poster:

JERSEYMEN! TO THE RESCUE!

Defend your country by nobly responding to its call. Young, able bodied and patriotic men are wanted immediately to fill up company D-12th regiment N.J. volunteers.

Col. Robt. C. Johnson

Each recruit, when sworn into service, will receive one month's pay in advance, and on being mustered into the service of the United States, will receive a bounty of $25. Every enlisted soldier who has a family or dependent widowed mother, will receive $6 a month as state pay, and upon his honorable discharge, a bounty of $75.

Single men, upon their honorable discharge, will receive $2 per month as state pay for the time they have been in service, and a bounty of $75.

Young Men, Come!

Volunteer at Once!

For further particulars inquire of Lieut. Edward S. Stratton,

Mustering Officer, Camp Stockton, Woodbury, NJ

An "ordinary " carpenter from Salem County, Charles Gamble, 34 years old answered his country's call of duty and volunteered for the currently forming 12th Regiment of New Jersey Volunteers Infantry. He would be leaving behind his beloved wife Elizabeth whom he had married March 26th, 1857.

This new regiment of 992 men was trained and "mustered in" September 4th at Camp Stockton, located on the Dickinson farm just outside of Woodbury, New Jersey.

The field and staff officers were chosen first, which included: Colonel Robert C. Johnson of Salem County, Lieutenant Colonel J. Howard Willetts of Cape May County, Major Thomas H. Davis of Cumberland County, Adjutant Henry C. Paxson, Quartermaster J. Frank Brown, Surgeon Alvin Satterhwaite, Assistant Surgeons Samuel T. Miller and Uriah Gilman and Chaplain William B. Otis.

The 12th New Jersey Infantry became so effective with their smoothbore .69 caliber Springfield muskets so loaded, that they became known as "The Buck and Ball Regiment." The brave and willing 12th New Jersey was also known as one of the most "fightingest" of all the regiments as they saw a lot of action in the war.

The raw rookies got their first shocking taste of war in The Battle of Chancellorsville from May 1-5, 1863, where Robert E. Lee's military skills overcame the Union's superior forces resulting in a significant Confederate victory. During the battle, the 12th suffered a loss of 179 killed, wounded or missing.

And then from July 1-3 they were involved in the bloodiest, costliest battle of the Civil War--Gettysburg--where there were over 50,000 casualties and about 7000 deaths. This battle was probably the turning point in the war for the Union as they stopped General Lee and the Confederate army from advancing any further north.

Of the original 992 eager young men who volunteered, only 278 valiant soldiers answered roll call when the 12th New Jersey were "mustered out" at the war's end in July, 1865.

These courageous men fought in fifty battles and skirmishes but they never surrendered their colors to the enemy.

Colonel J.Howard Willett

Colonel Robert C. Johnson

Major Thomas H. Davis

Alvin Satterhwaite, Surgeon

12th Regiment, New Jersey Volunteer Infantry

-----Organized at Camp Stockton, Woodbury, N.J., and mustered in September 4, 1862. Left State for Baltimore, Md., September 7, 1862. Attached to Defenses of Baltimore, Md. Unattached, 8th Army Corps, Middle Dept., to December, 1862. 2nd Brigade, 3rd Division, 2nd Army Corps, Army of the Potomac, to March, 1864. 3rd Brigade, 2nd Division, 2nd Army Corps, to July, 1865.

A chronological service log of the 12th Regiment which left the state for Baltimore, Maryland, September 7, 1862, is as follows:

- Guard duty at Ellicott's Mills, Md. Sept. 8, - Dec. 10, 1862
- Moved to Washington DC., December 10, thence to join army of the Potomac December 13-17, reporting at Falmouth, Va. December 20.
- Duty there till April 27, 1863
- Chancellorsville campaign April 27-May 6.
- Battle of Chancellorsville May 1-5
- Gettysburg (Pa.) Campaign June 11-July 24
- Battle of Gettysburg July 1-3, Pursuit of Lee to Manassas Gap July 5-24.
- Duty on Orange & Alexandria Railroad til September 12.
- Advance from the Rappahannock to the Rapidan September 13-17.
- Picket duty on the Rapidan til October
- Bristoe Campaign October 9-22
- Auburn and Bristoe October 14
- Advance to line of the Rappahannock November 7-8
- Mine Run Campaign November 26-December 2
- Mine Run November 28-30
- At Stevensburg till May 1864
- Demonstration on the Rapidan February 6-7
- Morton's Ford February-6-7
- Campaign from the Rapidan to the James May 3-June 15
- Battles of the Wilderness May 5-7;Laurel Hill May 8; Spotsylvania May 8-12; Po River May 10; Spotsylvania Court House May 12-21.

- Assault on the Salient, "Bloody Angel," May 12
- North Anna River May 23-26
- On line of the Pamunkey May 26-28.
- Totopotomoy May 28-31. Cold Harbor June 1-12.
- Before Petersburg June 16-18.
- Siege of Petersburg June 16, 1864 to April 2, 1865.
- Jerusalem Plank Road June 22-23, 1864
- Demonstration north of the James Aug. 13-20.
- Deep Bottom July 27-28.
- Demonstration north of the James Aug. 13-20.
- Strawberry Plains, Deep Bottom, Aug. 14-18.
- Ream's Station August 25.
- Boydton Plank Road, Hatcher's Run, Oct. 27-28.
- Dabney's Mills, Hatcher's Run, Feb. 5-7, 1865.
- Watkins House March 25.
- Appomattox Campaign March 28-April 9.
- Boydton & White Oak Roads March 30-31.
- Fall of Petersburg April 2.
- Pursuit of Lee April 3-9.
- Sailor's Creek April 6.
- High Bridge, Farmville, April 7.
- Appomattox Court House Apr 9. Surrender of Lee & His Army.
- March to Washington D.C., May 2-12.
- Grand Review May 23.
- Duty at Washington D.C. till July.
- Mustered out at Washington D.C., July 15, 1865.

Regiment lost during service 9 Officers and 168 Enlisted men killed and mortally wounded and 99 Enlisted men by disease. Total 276.

Letters

Woodbury, New Jersey c. 1860

Woodbury
August 29th, 1862.

Dear Parents;-

I take this present opportunity to write you to inform you that I am well at present and on guard today; I hate it though for we are going to have a big dinner today, but I can not help it. We take our turn when we are on duty.

Yesterday after we had been on our parade in the afternoon, Dave Smith had a hard fit, as hard a one as ever I saw and when he came too he did not know where he was and he asked me to take him home. I got him up and led him around a while and he found out where he was; when he found out where he was he asked me for something to drink and I had some and I gave him some whiskey. This morning he is all right except he is sorry.

We received our money for the month in advance, $13.00; and I have three notes on the Captain for about $15.00, and I think that I shall get it on Saturday.

It is pretty near time for me to go on duty, and I shall have to bring my letter to a close. Good-bye.

C. W. Gamble.

VIEW OF ELLICOTTS MILLS, MD

Ellicott's Mill, Maryland.
September 10th, 1862.

Dear Parents and Wife;-

I take the opportunity to sit down on a stone and make a desk of another one to write to you a few lines to inform you that I am well at present and hope that these few lines may find you all the same.

We are encamped on a hill in this place about 80 or 100 feet high and a valley all around. The Rebels are within 8 miles of us, and in fact they are all around us. Last night there was 5 of our Companies ordered out to the 14th Regiment about 12 o'clock on the double quick time; and that is about 5 mile from here. They have not returned yet with the exception of four men and they tired out and returned to their tents on the same night. Tonight I suppose that we will go out on the same errand by the looks of things and our officers around us. I think that we shall have to go in battle soon whether we are trained or not.

There is another Company (C) has just been called out and now I expect that our Company will have to go soon; they are all here at the fountain spring filling their canteens with water now: It is one of the best little streams of water that I ever saw. It runs out of a rock and is the best of water; it runs about an inch thick an about three feet from the rock.

I must stop and tell you about our travel out here; after we left Woodbury we went to Philadelphia and then we went into a place where we got a good dinner given us all, and then we marched to another *car**, about two miles and I tell you it was warm and I got tired of my baggage. When we got there I was as wet as if I had come out of a harvest field in July. We stayed there about an hour and then we started for Baltimore. We went through several places and crossed several rivers. We came to a place where we ran all of our cars on a boat at once and went across the river and there was a long string of them. Then we went on to Baltimore and we got there about 12 o'clock and then we got out of the cars and marched about 1 ½ miles to another car; there we (here I was called out to go out in the town and get our dress coats and tell you they are something handsome and I have just returned so now I will go on with the cars) got another good supper and then we all marched out on to the Rail-Road track and laid down on a stone pavement behind the railing and took our knapsacks for pillows and there we laid until morning.

Then we got aboard the cars about 10 o'clock and started and arrived here about 5 o'clock in the afternoon; then we marched up on this hill and laid down on our blankets and went to sleep. In the morning our tents came and we went to putting them up; and last night we rested right well in them until morning. No more at present but remain

Your Son and Husband
C. W. Gamble

Please read this letter to Eliza and give it to her. Henry Woodruff is well. Dave, Sam and all of the boys send their best respects to you all. Direct your letter to Baltimore County, Maryland, in care of Captain Moore Co. D 12th Regiment N. J. Volunteers.

Apparently the reference to "cars" refers to railroad cars.

4

Dear Parents and Wife;-

I take this opportunity to write to inform you that we are at the present at the same place where we were when last I wrote you. I am enjoying good health at present. I had a fit at Camp Stockton, and they said that it was a hard one; and I have been unwell ever since we have been here, and had another very hard fit, but I feel now as well as ever I felt in my entire life.

I often think of Eliza, my wife, and George and Father and Mother. I have been on *picket** duty once since I have been here; I was on about 30 hours and then returned to Camp again on Saturday the 12th about 11 o'clock. Then we had nothing to do only to attend to answer our names when the roll was called, so I went to the captain and got a pass for Dave and myself and went out in the town; there we went to a place and called for supper and we had a good one; we called for ham and eggs and we got it. They were good too, for they were rarity to us, for we have nothing here but boiled beef and those sea biscuits, and they are so hard as the rocks. Some times we have fried bacon and that is not extra and sometimes we have beans in soup. Today I see we are going to have some hominy for dinner, but I don't know whether I shall get any of it or not, for every one dips into it when ever he gets a chance. I should like for you to see us when meals are served; to see them with their dishes and cups, running like pigs to a trough for swill, and it is the best one that gets there first.

We have taken three of Jackson's men as prisoners, and have got them here in the guard-house; we had a hard time last night to keep the Cavalry off of them, and we have to put a guard around the tent to keep them from killing them, but to day they have left here for

Baltimore. I tell you they are a hard looking set; they are a harder looking set than we are, and that is needless.

To day and Sunday we had a chance to go to meeting, but we thought that we would write home. So we, Dave and myself, went down to our stone desk and commenced to write home letters to you all.

All the butter, eggs and bread that we get here we have to pay for out of our own pockets, and that is very hard; we have to pay .25 a dozen for eggs; .25 for butter and .10 for a loaf of bread, and it takes off the money very fast; but to day they have brought in some bread. So no more at present, but remain

Your Son
C. W. Gamble.

P.S. Henry Woodard and Sam Green are well and in good spirits and send their best respects to you all. Write soon and let me know how you are getting along. Direct your letters to me at Ellicott's Mills, Baltimore County, Md. 12ᵗʰ Regiment.

*** Picket** - *An advance outpost or guard for a large force. Ordered to form a scattered line far in advance of the main army's encampment, but within supporting distance, a picket guard was made up of a lieutenant, 2 sergeants, 4 corporals, and 40 privates from each regiment. Picket duty constituted the most hazardous work of infantrymen in the field. Being the first to feel any major enemy movement, they were also the first liable to be killed, wounded, or captured. And the most likely targets of snipers.*
Source: (www.civilwarhome.com)

Camp Johnson, Maryland
September 25th, 1862

Dear Parents and Wife;-

I take my pen in hand to write to you to inform you that I am well at present and hope that these few lines will find you the same. I said that I would write no more letters to you; I have written two letters to you since I have been here and have not yet received any answer. I think very hard of you for not writing to me if you have received them; if you did not receive them I will excuse you; I tell you that I want to hear from home; I want to hear how Eliza and George are getting along and all the rest of you.

I stated in my other letter all about from the time that we left Woodbury until we arrived here. We have nothing to do here at present but go out on picket and guard and drill once or twice in a day. When we go out on picket we stay 24 hours, and when we are on guard we stay 24 hours and then we come off and the next day we can get a pass to go out in the town until 6 o'clock; and the next day we are put on police duty – that is to clean up the streets between the tents. When we go on guard we are put on in alphabetical order and every one takes his turn according to his name.

Dave Smith has been under the Doctor's hands for about ten days; he says that he has got the inflamtory rheumatism in his legs. The rest of our boys are well at present.

There is 13 in our tent, and we now cook for ourselves. We cook our meals in Jersey style now and we find that we can eat it a great deal better and it agrees with us better. We have no butter or pepper here unless we find it ourselves. Dave and I got a pass the other day and went out and got butter for ourselves. Dave and myself sleep side by side and what one has the other has too. Sometimes we get some whiskey and we divide it too. Henry Woodard sleeps on the other side of Dave. Yesterday he went out on a pass and he came in pretty tight but he is over it now and he says that he is in notion not to drink any more of the dam stuff, because it makes such a dam fool of him.

There was about 12,000 or 15,000 Rebel prisoners here on Saturday from Harpers Ferry and Fredericksburg; we had to guard them while they were here until they left for Annapolis where they are at present. There has been several thousand Rebel prisoners pass through here in the cars but none of them stopped here. They were guarded by our Company here; we all marched out in the road and seen them pass. They were the dirtiest looking men that I ever saw in my life. They had no uniform whatever. When the cars stopped some of our boys hurrahed for Johnson and they hurrahed for Jackson. I tell you I felt like ramming bayonets through them. Their officers looked as bad as the soldiers did.

I must stop now. Read this letter to Eliza and let her have it and tell her to keep it and all the rest that she gets. Write to me as quick as you get this letter and let me know whether you got the rest or not. Good-bye,

From Your Son and Husband
C. W. Gamble.

Camp Johnson,
Ellicott's Mills, Maryland.
October 5th, 1862.

Dear Parents and Wife;-

I now sit down to write you to inform you that I am well yet and enjoying good health and hope that you are all the same. I received your letter and that tea on October 2nd and it was dated the 15th of September and I was pleased to read it as the Court-Marshall of Dan Ward by Captain Joseph Garton was in it. I called all the boys of Pittstown in to the tent and read it to them and I tell you that they had some hearty laughs over it and when I was through reading it they gave three cheers for Captain Garton and said they would have liked to have been there.

Father we now begin to have a little harder work to do. The whole regiment has to march about three miles to drill and all of us together; and the road is so dusty when you are at one end you can not see the other as we have not had any rain here of any amount since we have been here; and the road that we travel is all the way up hill when we go out to drill and about half the way up when we come back to camp. They give us double quick time and when we get into camp our hair whiskers and clothes are all of one color and we all have to go down to the run and take a good wash before we can feel anything like ourselves and it makes me feel tired. We get in about 2 o'clock and then some times we have a little whiskey and then we take a small drink; then we have a good appetite for our dinner.

Last Sunday morning the whole Regiment was called out in one line and that was a long string of us to hear the laws and rules read to us, and all so the Court-Marshall of three of our privates. One of them has to carry a barrel on his neck for one week and live on nothing but bread and water. The way the barrel is fixed is one head knocked out and the other has a square hole cut in it about 8 inches

9

just big enough to let his head through. He has to go up and down all of our streets in camp twice a day; his crime was for breaking open a trunk.

One is to carry his knapsack filled with stones 2 hours every day for one week and lose one months pay and live on bread and water; his crime is for shooting at one of the privates; and the other is to be brought before the guard-house every day for 2 hours for one week and live on bread and water as they belong to our Regiment I will not expose them by telling their names.

On Monday I was out on the R.R. at Winchester on picket about 4 miles from camp guarding the switches as some of them had been turned as they supposed by the Rebs so we have to guard them day and night. We go out in the morning and stay there until the next morning and then we are relieved by another Company. Our Company goes on once a week. On Monday night and Tuesday there was 13 trains of cars passed here; they had from 25 to 30 cars on each train and they were all full inside and on top. Supposed to be 30,000 or 40,000 they were going down the Potomac we supposed. They made such a hollering that you could hardly hear yourself talk.

Tuesday we came off of picket about 2 o'clock and then we had nothing to do but clean our guns and equipment and cook our supper. Every night about 9 o'clock we are all each Company called out in line to answer to our names and then at the tap of the drum we blow out our lights and go to bed as we call it. Wednesday we had to march out on our ground to drill again and it was as dusty as ever. Thursday, Friday, and Saturday we were out on guard on the bridge in town and stayed until morning. This Sunday is pleasant as it rained on Saturday night and laid the dust pretty well.

Last week we had the Court marshall of another one of our privates; he has to be drummed up and down the streets of our camp twice a day with a board before and behind and on it in big letters lose one months pay and live on nothing but bread and water for one week. His crime was stealing money from other soldiers.

10

Money is getting scarce with us here as we have to pay the highest price for everything that we get. I am out as I did not keep much with me and our Captain says he don't think we shall get any for three months and I do not know how I shall get along till then for it has cost me about $2.00 a week to get my washing done for we have to keep ourselves clean according to the rules of our camp. I have to get three shirts and two pairs of drawers washed a week and have to pay .12 a piece for them and my tobacco and other things cost me about $2.00 a week.

I sent Eliza a certificate so that she can draw her State money; tell her to take care of it and not lose it, but she can draw her money from Salem when she wants it. That is $6.00 a month; she has got some coming to her now. Lize if you have not spent all the money that I let you have sent me a little and when I draw my wages I will send them to you.

Father I saw John Loper yesterday and he told me that he was coming to Pittstown and I send by him three cartridges to you and two caps such as we use. Father come up and see us it won't cost you but about $10.00 here and back and you can stay here with us and it won't cost you a cent and you won't begrudge your money just to see how we are situated.

Yesterday there was a hearse with a coffin in it and word come to us while we were on guard that the coffin had fire arms in it; it was for some of the Rebs; I saw it when it passed but did not think but what it was a corpse but what will the Rebs do if they have got to carrying their arms in a coffin. No more at present but remain

Your Son and Husband
C. W. Gamble.
Good Bye.

Camp Johnson,
Ellicott's Mills, Md.
October 16th, 1862

To My Dear Parents and Wife;-

I now sit down to scratch you a few lines to let you know that I received your letter on the 14th and the money that you sent me, and was glad to hear that you were all well. I am enjoying good health at present and hope that this letter may find you all enjoying the same good health.

We had just come off of a Company drill when I was informed that there was a letter for me and I got it and read it, and was pleased to hear from home. While I was opening my letter Sam came in with one from his Mother for me to read, and he was pleased to hear from her.

We have had some rain here since I wrote my last letter and it makes it very pleasant for us to drill now; it was quite muddy and slippery the next morning after the rain and when we went up and down the hill we had to mind how we walked or else the hind part of our pantaloons would kiss the ground; I looked pretty well for my own part for I did not get a fall, but I saw several of our boys with their pants quite muddy on the seat of them. But after one day it was quite smoother and nice for us to march on with the exception of the stones and I found that the rain had not softened them any.

Yesterday some of our officer's wives came to see them and we had to go out and drill as they wanted to see us all on drill and we did not get in until nearly dark and we had no time to cook any supper so we took the bean soup that was left from dinner. In the morning Dave, Henry, and myself got up about daybreak and built a fire and went to cooking breakfast: you ought to have been here to see us cook; one of us was frying beef and one cutting wood and punching fire and the other making coffee in a pot about 15 inches long and 9 inches in diameter and that was full too. After we got up to our tent you ought to have seen them coming with their cups and plates after coffee and fried beef and bread. Some of them were like pigs going to a trough, as Some of them are too lazy to cook and can not get out of their beds until some one gets the meals ready for them.

Father I was out on picket the other day about 7 miles from here and was scouting about through the woods and I saw a tree that had leaves on that looked like an orange tree and I went to it and it had something on it that looked to me like lemons; they were just the shape of them and I got some of them and they smelled just like oranges, but I did not taste them until I got back to the orange grove where we were on picket. Then I asked the miller of the mill (his name was Gamble) what they were and he told me that they were paw-paws and that they were good to eat when ripe and good to fry when about half ripe; some of them that I had were ripe and they ate them quick: I tasted them but they were too sweet for me, and I did not like them much. They told me that the seed would come up if planted so I saved some of them and send them to you for to plant and see what they will do.

Last Sunday I got a pass and had a good tramp around on the tops of some of the high hills around here. Some of the farms have so many stones on them that I do not know how they can farm them, but they told me that they could raise good grain and grass. I will send you some of my passes so you can see how we have to get out.

When you write let me know whether Eliza got her certificate or not and let me know whether you got my tools and chest from John's or not. I have not received the Sunbeam yet. We shall have to go on drill now so I'll stop for the present.

I will now commence again; if you have not got my chest tell John to bring it to my house and leave it and the boring machine with it and see that all of my tools are in it. Tell Eliza not to lend them but if you want them go to her and she will let you have them. Today I received the Sunbeam that you sent me and was glad to get it.

13

One of our brother soldiers died this morning; his name was Thomas McRithen (James McRithen's son) and we had a funeral march in our camp. Today we marched out to the cars with him in the coffin to send him home to Williamstown. It does seem very solemn to see one of our soldiers march out of camp in a coffin and it made us feel so to for we do not know how soon one of us may have to be carried the same way. Our regiment pays the very best respects to the funeral of one of our brother soldiers and I am not the least afraid if I was taken sick and died here but what I would be taken care of and sent home.

Father we expect to stay here all winter but not in our tents. We have got the cotton factory to move in. It is about 300 yards from our camp so we shall not have far to move. The building is not in operation now and it is five stories high and built of stone and has heaters all over it and that will make it comfortable for us. They are going to take the inside work out soon and I do not know when we shall move. Tell Lize to write me soon and tell me how to direct my letter and I will write to her. So good bye till I see you all,

C. W. Gamble.

Camp Johnson,
Ellicott's Mills, Md.
October 30th, 1862

To my dear and Affectionate Wife and Parents;-

I now sit down to drop you a few lines to inform you that I received your loving letter and was glad to hear that you all were enjoying such good health. Your letter found me in good health with the exception of a cold and that gave me a cold in the breast which makes me feel a little uncomfortable at present; but I am in hopes that I will be relieved of that in a few days, I have not been under the Doctor's hands yet, nor have not taken any of his medicine yet, nor neither do I want to take any of it as long as my health will permit me to; several of our soldiers have been taking his medicine and they say that he makes them worse instead of better. We have several sick soldiers in the hospitals now, and some I don't think will ever get home again. The weather has got so cold here in camp that they have moved the hospital down in the town in a dwelling house, which makes it a great deal better and warmer for them these cool nights and damp weather, for we have had some bitter cold nights and damp weather here.

It commenced raining here last Saturday morning and rained on until Monday morning about 10 o'clock and then it cleared off very nice and has remained so until the present time; I was out on guard at the time of the rain and not having no oil cloth coat or blanket I got wringing wet and that is the way that I got my cold and if I could get myself a coat or blanket I would get one as they will keep the rain off of us; the overcoats that we have keep off some of the rain but when you have to be out in the rain eight and ten hours, and they get so wet that they are as heavy almost as led and then have to lay down in them on nothing but straw and sometimes on bare ground it is a wonder that there is no more sick than there is; as for my own part I have enjoyed good health since I have been here with the exception of the cold that I speak about and have gained in my

15

weight 12 lbs. up to the present time and they all tell me that I am getting as fat as any one in the regiment, but I can not tell how soon I may take a change, but I still hope that I may have the same good health as I have had since I have been in the regiment.

There is one thing if I should live to get home I shall have the biggest pair of whiskers you ever saw me wear as I have not shaved since I have been here and Eliza is not here to shave me nor to cut them off now, but if I should live to get home and my wife Eliza should see me there she may have a chance to shave me again and I do hope that we, both of us, and all the rest of you may live to see one another again and enjoy the comforts we have enjoyed together.

Tell Eliza to take good care of George, and use him well for my sake, and likewise herself until I do get home and not let him starve nor starve herself either; as I want him and her to have enough to eat and wear until I do come home that is if I should live to go home.

Our captain and one of our orderlies have been home on a furlough and one of our corporals and they all overstayed their time and the colonel ordered them all to be under arrest; they came home today and our lieutenant notified them of the case and our captain did not like it and he has started down into the town to see the colonel about it and I do not know how they will make it, but they seem to think that the stripes will have to come off of the orderly and the corporal and that it will go pretty hard with the captain but I hope it may not be the case.

Our pay roll came in day before yesterday and today we are all called on to sign it; I have just been and signed it and I had to write my name in three different places and write it very fine at that. I do not know when we shall get our money some say that we will get it in ten days and some say not until one month but I can not tell when they will pay but one thing I know there is some of the boys that will not have much coming to them as there is a sutlers* tent here as they call it and they can draw orders from the captain and get what they want by paying two prices for them; they buy apples for 50

16

cents a bushel and sell them out for one and two cents a piece; pies for ten cents; worth about three cents and all other things according to the price of the things that I have above mentioned but as for my own part I have not took up one cent of my wages and have not spent over 50 cents with me so I have all of my wages coming to me.

I stated when I wrote home before that we expected to move down in the town, but I don't know whether we shall go there now; there is a talk of us having to move from here to some other place all together but I can not tell any thing about it for I do not believe that there is any of us knows any thing about it, what we shall do yet; not even one of our officers without it is some of our head ones. They have took twelve of our privates out of the regiment to cut wood for us this winter; but what place we are to burn it I cannot say as yet: they are cutting it about five miles from the camp.

As you stated in your letter that you were getting along with the house pretty smart and you wanted to lathe and plaster it before Eliza moved, I think it would be the best if you could get to do it. George Sithens promised to get me the plastering lathe for the house and I saw him the other day about it and he told me that the water was so low that they were not sawing much down there now but there would be some there after a while, and if there is any there I would like to get them there as he owes me and that will save paying the money for them; and lime and anything you can get where they owe me get them to get anything that you can. Before you plaster it up stairs I want collar beams put across over head, something like 2 by 5 of one inch board on each side of the rafter with a strip nailed to the board up the side to the peak of the rafter and before putting the collar beams up I would like you to draw the planks in to gather as you will see they are sprung out and that makes a hollow in the peak of the roof.

Now I will have to stop for this time; write and tell me how Kate and Taylor comes on: take Kate and go hunting with her as the season has come in, but don't let anyone have her without you are along. Write as soon as you can make it convenient and let me know how you are getting along. Good-bye

From Your Son and Husband—C. W. Gamble

* Sutlers - A common sight in the camps of Civil War soldiers was a string of huts or tents bulging with various items for sale. These business establishments belonged to sutlers, civilians officially appointed to supply soldiers with a long list of approved items. In both the Union and Confederate armies each regiment was allowed 1 sutler. From these camp vendors a soldier could purchase such items as food, newspapers, books, tobacco, razors, tin plates, cups, cutlery, and illegal alcohol.

Source: www.civilwarhome.com

Civil War Sutler

Camp Johnson, Maryland
December 10, '62.

Dear Parents and Wife;-

I take my pen in hand to inform you that I received your kind and welcome letter last night and one from Charlie Hitchner. I have not time to write much for we have got orders to move and there is a Company waiting to take our place and we are all in a flustercation; I can hardly write. I hate to leave here now since we have got our tents fixed, but we have to go this morning to Washington, and we can not tell where we shall go next, but they tell me that we are going in battle. You need not write to me again till you hear from me again. Tell Hite not to come to Ellicott's Mills but to come to Washington and then he can tell where we are; and I want him to follow the regiment if he can. Send the box to Washington and it will be sent to me. Father I have not much time to write; we have to start now; right away.

From Your Son
C. W. Gamble.

Tell Lib Smith that Dave is on duty and has not got time to write until we get moved and then he will write right away.

Springfield 69 Caliber Rifle

Washington, December 11, '62

Dear Father Mother and Wife;-

I now sit down to write you a few lines to inform you that I am well at present, but I am tired to day and my shoulders ache from carrying my knapsack. I hope that these few lines will find you all enjoying good health. Well Father we did leave Ellicott's Mills the tenth of the month. I commenced this letter yesterday the 11th and now I will try to finish it.

We are here at Washington yet, but expect to leave every minute. We marched down to the Armory last night to get our guns changed but it was too late to get them; and we had to make another expedition to day for them. We can not tell whether we shall get them changed or not, but we expect to get them changed before we leave here. Our Captain says that we have to go to Virginia or a place about 65 miles from here; and he says that he thinks that we will have to march all the way there if they don't get a steamer to take us. The march will be a hard job for us for the mud here around Washington is about six inches deep and it is like mortar.

Father, Washington is a nice place if it wasn't so muddy; I have seen the Capitol and have been all around it. I have seen Richard Robison and Daniel and Walter Sheets and several others since I have been here. We are all together, the whole regiment in one house and have plenty of room to drill in it. We are waiting to get the command to go. Our fellows seem to be enjoying themselves very well at present. Dave got out of the cars when we got here and we did not see any more of him till about 2 o'clock this morning and then he came in and hollered for me. I heard him and waked up and spoke to him, and asked him what he wanted and where he had been; he told me that he had been to Georgetown and then we both laid down and went to sleep, and this morning he got up and I helped him roll up his blanket and then he cleared out again and I saw him no more until this afternoon; then him and Dick Robinson came to me while I was on duty; and he was a little tight; and he told me that he was going to join the regulars and wanted me to go with him. I told him no. Then he started off and I have not seen him since.

Father we got one months pay to day and that was all. I had to pay $6.00 for my boots and $100.00 towards the stone and I was going away I didn't know where I thought that I might stand in need of the rest for I did not know what might turn up, so I shall not send any home this time. Father, Mother and Wife I don't know when I shall get home now. Don't look for me until you see me. Try and take good care of yourselves and my wife and George till I do come and I will try and recompense you for it if I live. It is almost time for me to go on duty I must stop writing. Good-bye

> From Your Son and Husband
> C. W. Gamble.

When we get settled down I will write again. When you write direct to Washington and it will follow the regiment (in care of Captain Moore)

Dear Parents and Wife;-

I now take my pen in hand to inform you that I am well and am on the land and among the living and I hope that these few lines will find you enjoying good health. I wrote you a letter while I was in Washington which I suppose that you have received.

I will now endeavor to tell you our travels to Virginia; we started from Washington on the 14th to Liverpool Point about ten o'clock and marched about twelve miles where we stopped for the night. The mud on the road was about six inches deep and we had to ford runs about 12 inches deep. When we would stop to rest our boys would lighten their knapsacks by throwing out pants, drawers, shirts, and trousers and some even threw away their blankets and some their whole knapsacks. I suppose that not less than a 100 pair of pants were left on the road.

When we stopped we took some grub and built fires and rolled up in our blankets and laid down for the night on the ground. There was a cavalry put up with us and there was several boys among them that we knew; among them was Charles Thomas, Bill's brother. In the morning we ate our breakfasts it being on the 15th and we started on our journey being stiff and sore we did not go very fast. We cook our meat by putting it on the sharp end of a stick and holding it before the fire.

We marched on until we came to a town called Scataway; the first town that we had seen since we left Washington. We got here about 12 o'clock where we eat our grub and then we started on until we came to another place in the woods where we put up for the night. In the morning the 16th we started on again and the road was still muddy and no houses on the road but we could see some from the road and corn stalk stables and there were woods all of the way, and principally spruce pine some places there was large timber; it being in marshy land. We marched on till about sunset when we come to a place where we put up for the night and then it came my turn to go out on guard which I dreaded but had to do my duty.

We encamped in a very low place. About 5 o'clock on the 17th it commenced raining very hard and our camp was all covered with water; some of the boys laid in it but we eat our grub and started on the road being muddier than ever, but we traveled on it being our last days travel in Maryland. We marched on until we came to a place in the Potomac River called Fair Point where we stopped. In the morning on the 18th our wagons came with our tents and we were ordered to put them up; we had not more than got to work at them before we had orders to strike tents then we took them down and packed them up again and took them down to the steamboat wharf and put them on board and then we marched down and went on board and landed in Virginia. It was snowing all the time.

When we got across we marched about 1 mile to a hill called Leed's Hill where we put up for the night. The next morning being the 19th we eat our grub again and then they drove in 6 beeve and in the afternoon they butchered one of them and we had beef for supper and breakfast and after breakfast we started in again driving the other 5 beeves with us. Dave and myself being a little behind we took to the Rail Road it being the best way and the best walking and went well enough till we got within 2 miles of where we encamped where we ran afoul of a provost guard and he stops us and we had to wait until he went to his captain to get permission to let us pass and then we went on and joined our regiment just as it got in camp where we now are.

The next morning we ate our grub and then we killed 2 more of our beeves then we had beef again; then we went and seen the boys of the 24th. John Simpkins, Henry Hughes, William Ackley and his son Frank and several others. Our tents not being here we had to make tents out of pine it being night. Dave, Henry Woodruff and Joel Abbott and myself put up in one tent and slept very

23

comfortable for the night. This morning being the 20th our tents come and we are now putting them up; since I commenced this letter George Green has come over and is now here with us and he looks as hearty as a buck, but he is like the rest of us he is pretty well smoked with this Virginia pine. We expect to be stockadeed in with the 2th and others so us Jersey boys will all be together.

We are now within 2 miles of the Rebs and can see their batteries in the town of Fredericksburg. I do not suppose that is worth while to tell you anything about the battle that was fought last; I expect that you know all about it, but I tell you I have seen the effects of it in the 24th: some of their guns all broke to pieces and some have got no blankets nor tents and no clothes but what they have got on; to hear them tell of the battle and hardships they have been through it is enough to make us tremble. But if we are called to go in a fight I am going to endeavor to do my little might while life shall last as I think that I am in a just cause and that it is all right so Good-bye

C. W. Gamble

Direct your letters to Washington to follow the Regiment Co. D. 12th Regiment N. J. Vol. Sam Green Gaskill and all of the rest of the boys are well.

Fredericksburg

24

Falmouth, Virginia.
January 10, 1863.

Dear Parents and Wife;-

I take my pencil in hand to write you to let you know that I received your letter dated the 4th, and was pleased to hear from home and to hear that you were all well and to hear that Eliza was so comfortable in her new house. I must say that when I get a letter from home it does me almost as much good as if I was at home to see what is going on myself.

I have enjoyed very good health since I have been here until now I have got the bowel complaint or something like it which keeps me running night and day and that makes it uncomfortable for me. Dave had the same complaint a few days back but he has gotten very nearly over it so that he does not have to get up nights. I hope that these few lines may find you all in good health.

I do not know that I can tell you anything new that is going on in the army but I will endeavor to say something. We have had it very mild here with the exception of two or three days and they were pretty cold days and nights. I was on guard one of the nights and we had to keep fires all night on our beats in order to keep warm. We have some pretty tough times once in a while and some good times too but we must expect it in a soldiers life; but when we go over in the other regiments and see how they are cut up and see and hear them tell how they have fared, we can come back to our tents and feel very well satisfied. We have had to live on hardtack as we could get them ever since we left Ellicott's Mills till yesterday when we drew bread; each one of us draw a loaf a day and that loaf is to last us three meals but Sam Green says that he can eat a loaf at a meal and some times he does it and goes without the other two, but he can take down every thing in our tent. When he was around Pittstown he never had much to say but here he is one of the wildest boys in the regiment. It is almost impossible to keep him still night or day asleep or awake.

I have seen George several times since I have been here. When we go out to see them that we are acquainted with it seems almost as if we were at home paying visits; but we do not want to stay long as we all want to get back to our own regiment as it seems the most like home to us.

It is raining here to day and some of us are sitting round our new fire place with a good fire in it and some are out cutting wood. I have been down to the Falmouth since I wrote you my last letter and saw the place and a hard looking place it is too. It looks as if it had seen some very rough times; some of the brick houses with all of the wood work burnt out and nothing standing but the walls and no fences to be seen any where. Falmouth lays on the same side of the river that we are on and Fredericksburg on the other side; the distance across is less than a quarter of a mile but the town lies a little south of Falmouth. I saw several rebels on the other side of the river. Our pickets are on this side guarding the other side and they are within hearing of one another.

It is dinner time now and I must stop and cook Dave's and my dinner. I do the cooking and Dave washes the dishes. The way we fry our meat we take our plate and get a stick and split one end and put it across the edge of the plate and that makes the handle. I wish Lize and the rest of you could be here to see us cook. I saw several brick houses in Fredericksburg with the wood work all burnt out and musket holes through the walls which our boys had done and it was a sight for me and if I ever do live to get home I shall have something to tell you all. I will have to stop so good bye Dad.

From Your Son
C. W. Gamble.

Write right away and don't neglect it. Dave is writing home too.
This is the plan that I studied out to fix a fire place in our tent which we find it handy for us to cook by and all of us can get around the

fire at one time and at night we all lay with our feet to the fire. There has been several of our boys to look at it and they are fixing theirs the same way. It is composed of 4 poles set in the ground about three feet and pieces set across the top which leaves it all open around the sides; and then we made a stick chimney and plastered it with clay inside and out and it does fine I tell you. We took the poles out of the center and took three poles like shears and fastened the ends together and fastened the chain of our tent and fastened the poles and the tent all up together which makes it stand steadier and firmer; if the rest blows down ours will be a standing.

I will try to fill this up. Tell Eliza that I would like for her to dig up them quince bushes and peach trees and currant bushes where she moved from and set them out in the lot where she thinks would be the best place for them; and take them up right away if she can or before the 1st of March as David Hitchner told me I could take them away when I put them there. Dig some of them artichokes and put them in the lot. If I should live to get home again I would like to have them. Father I would like for you to write every week as we are so far apart I want to hear from home. Tell Dave DuBois that I will write to him soon and look out for it. Good-bye

C. W. Gamble.

Battlefield Post Office at Falmouth

Camp Near Falmouth, Virginia.
January 12th, 1863.

Dear Brother and Sister;-

I now take my pencil in hand to inform you that I received your letter and was glad to hear from you and your family once more and to hear that you were all well with the exception of colds for we are all liable to have them. I have enjoyed good health since I have been in the service until now, I have the bowel complaint or some thing like it, for three days which makes me feel very weak at present but I am in hope that I will be over it in a few days.

While we were at Ellicott's Mills we were comfortably fixed in our tents and we had flowers in there, floor in there and they were boarded up the sides; there were 15 in a tent and we joined and bought stores and were living comfortable in them, new bread every day and good beef and pork and plenty of it and all were satisfied with it. But as soon as we got fixed we had orders to leave.

We left there on the 10th of December and arrived at Washington that night in the cars and was there 3 nights and 2 days and then we got our guns changed; in the morning we started on our march for Liverpool Point about 60 miles from Washington which we marched in 3 ½ days, and the roads were very muddy some times they were 6 or 7 inches deep which made it bad for us, but I got along very well. I bought me a pair of high leg boots and I found them to be of great service to me; the first day we marched our boys commenced to lighten their knapsacks by throwing away their pants, shirts, coats, and blankets and some their boots and some their whole knapsacks but I stuck to mine and did not throw away anything; and carried a flag that was made a present to the Company at Ellicott's Mills a head of the Company.

We would travel all day and at night we would roll up in our blankets and lay down on the ground for the night; in the morning we would feel very stiff but had to march on. At last we got to our journey's end and a tired set we were too when we got there and we did not get there until dark. The next morning we were ordered to put up our tents which we went to work to do and got them pretty nearly up when we had orders to strike tents. We then took them down and we packed them up and put them in the wagons and marched to the steamboat and went on board and landed in Virginia and it snowed all the time.

After we got across we marched about a mile to a place called Leed's Hill where we stayed 2 nights and 1 day; then we started on our march again and landed where we are now. The day we laid at Leed's Hill they drove in 6 beeves and they killed one of them and we had beef again. If I had been home and saw a beef killed the way they did that one I could not have eaten a bit of it but as it was it was good enough, and they baked it on the ground.

We see some rough times here once in a while and some nice times too; but when we go over to the 24th regiment and others that have been in battle we come back to our own and are well contented with our own fare. They brought our stores as far as Washington and there they said that they were too heavy to cart in their wagons so they throwed them out and so we have no stores now. I studied a plan out to rig a fire in our tent and we have our fire place now which makes it quite comfortable now.

We are close to the Rebs and do not know how soon we may be in battle, nor we do not know how soon we may have to leave as we are under marching orders and have been ready for several days. But I am ready to move when ever called on but I hate to leave our tents as they are Sibley tents and 15 of us can put up in them, that is in one of them and they will turn rain. When we move we have to take these little tents with us; they are intended for 2 to take together and to build together and we have got them now and they are nothing more than common muslin and rain goes right through them very easy which makes it not so pleasant for us.

Annie you said in your letter that you were glad that you had a brother that would volunteer in the war for his country. My Country is what caused me to leave my wife and parents and friends and it is the Country that my fore fathers fought for and I thought that it was a just cause or I would not have been here to day. I felt it my duty to do it and if it should be my lot to live through it I shall have something to tell you and all the rest of my friends. I feel contented when I am well and can hear from home and hear that they are all well; but when I am unwell my mind is on home all of the time.

I have been down and seen Fredericksburg and saw the Rebs on the other side of the river; our pickets guard this side of the river and the Rebs the other and they can hollar to one another so they can be distinctly heard. You wanted to know whether I had an oil cloth coat or blanket; I have not got one as I did not know what I wanted when I was where I could get one for we cannot get anything of the kind here. Well I must close by saying Good-bye

From Your Brother
C. W. Gamble.

Write to me soon and as often as you can and I will answer. This is my first to you and you must excuse me for not writing before. I have seen George Green and several others that I know since I have been here. Write right away.

*The **Sibley tent** was invented by the American military officer Henry Hopkins Sibley*

Of conical design, it stands about twelve feet high and eighteen feet in diameter. It can comfortably house about a dozen men.

Falmouth, Virginia
January 20th, 1863

Dear Parents and Wife;-

I now take my pencil in hand to inform you that I received your letter to day dated the 17th, and was glad to hear from you and to hear that you were all well; your letter found me in very good health now that I have gotten over the bowel complaint.

They have detailed me out for a cook and I am now exempt from all duty as long as I am cook. I begin to think that there is some thing going to be done soon; for there has been to day a general review of the whole brigade and I think that we will be in battle soon if we are going to fight at all for it looks more like it every day, and in fact, every hour. We have not gone yet, but tomorrow morning we may be gone from here. We have to have three days rations cooked ahead and to have everything packed up so as to be ready to start when we are called on.

There has been 100 12 lbs guns drawn past here this afternoon; each one was drawn by six horses. Our orders have just been read to us that we have got to cross the Rappahannock and to clean our guns and get ready for a fight with the enemy. Some of our boys in the regiment hurrahs and dances to think that they are going in a battle, but I think that some of them may get enough of it before they get through. I don't feel very anxious for my own part but I come out for that purpose and I don't feel worried about it; if I get in a battle I shall endeavor to do the best that I can while life shall last. The artillery have been going by here for 2 hours and are still going by.

Our Lieutenant says that we have to go to-morrow. Since I commenced to cook I have to stay down at the cook tent to watch it and have to sleep along; we keep all the provision in the tent with me and I have to attend to it myself. So Dave and I have to part nights now, but we are together days. Dave find a good deal of fault 'cause he don't get any letters; he wants you to put his wife in the humor for writing. I am cooking now and have to go out and look at my fire about every 2 or 3 lines but I have to eat and so have to attend to it.

The $17.00 that is behind on rent with D. Hitchner, I do not know now what it is for but it is on the book and you can tell. This last year is one by $20.00 a year and you can tell what the whole is. Tell him to wait a while if he can and I will pay him the balance with interest; tell him I think hard if he won't let me take them trees that I set out there for he told me if I wanted them when I moved I could have them or I would have set them out on my own lot. I must close by saying good-bye,

Your Son and Husband,
C. W. Gamble.

Direct as before and they will follow the regiment. I received a letter from Annie and have written her an answer. C. W. G.

Federal cavalry column along the Rappahannock River, Virginia

Falmouth, Virginia.
February 2nd, 1863

Dear Brother and Sister;-

I now take my pencil in hand to inform you that I received your kind and welcome letter on the 30th of last month and was pleased to hear from you, but was sorry to hear that you had sore eyes; I have had them for some time so that I have to wet my finger every morning and rub my eyes before I can get them open. They detailed me out to cook for the Company and this Virginia pine smoke don't help them any and if you were to see me you would think I was cooked too as the smoke has changed my color so much.

I have about 70 to cook for and it keeps me busy all the time; I have been at it about 2 weeks and I believe it agrees with me better than to do my duties as a soldier as I am excused from duty while I am cook. It is more exercise for me to cook and I think that it is better for me; but the one that cooks has a good deal to contend with and a man has to have a great deal of patience as I have so many to wait on at meal time. What I have to cook is to boil pork and make coffee and tea once a week and we have fresh beef once a week and that I sometimes boil and deal it out to them and sometimes I cut off steaks one a piece for each man and they fry it in their tin plates by taking a stick about 2 feet long and splitting one end of it and put it a straddle of it across the edge of the plate and holding it over the fire; it answers very well for us. We have beans which I make soup of and sometimes we have other vegetables. Sometimes we have this vegetable cheese to make soup of. I expect that you know what that is and if you don't I will endeavor to tell you what it is composed of; it is composed of cabbage, carrots, turnips, potatoes, and other vegetables dried, and when I cook it I pour boiling water on it and soak it about a half an hour and then I put it in the pot and then I put a little rice in it and a piece of pork to season it and it makes good soup. We draw bread for one day in the week and the

34

rest of the time we have to eat hardtack called army bread. They find us salt but no pepper to put on grub we have to find that ourselves when we can get it but we cannot get that now.

I will now stop telling you about my cooking affairs and tell you a little about the way the weather has been here; we have had plenty of rain since we have been here and on the 28th it snowed all day and night and a bad storm it was too and it made it bad for our guards and pickets to be out in but they had to be out in it for there is no backing out here, we have it to do. It has made the roads bad here, in fact, so bad that it is almost impossible to travel them. 6 horses cannot draw more than 600 lbs. weight on the roads. They undertook to take three pontoons by here to cross the Rappahannock but could not get them there so they had to turn back and they all say that they are in sight of our camp now and they say that they cannot move them now on account of the roads.

You state that you would like to send me a box if we should stay here; I think that we shall stay here some time now but I do not know whether you can get a box here or not. It might come and it might not although some get boxes here. You said that you would like to send me a coat or blanket it is very kind of you but it would not be worth while now as the winter is nearly over and as we have to travel it would make my load heavy for me to carry but as for the box of knick-knacks I would be glad to have them if I thought they would get here safe and it would not make any difference what kind of knick-knacks they were for anything would taste good here that came from Jersey.

When we encamped here the camp was in the wood and there was plenty of wood here and now there is no timber to be seen within a mile around us; it has been all cut off for wood and we have to cut and carry wood for a mile now as the teams cannot cart it as fast as we can use it on account of the roads being so bad.

Well I have forgot to tell you about my health. I am enjoying as good health now as I have since I left Ellicott's Mills. I am in good health and I hope that these few lines will find you all the same.

35

Samuel Green is now sick and we had to take him to the hospital; but he is getting better now. Dave Smith sends his respects to you both. Well I must close as it is getting time for the drum to tap to blow out the lights so good-bye Brother and Sister. Excuse writing and paper as this is all that I have got and I am in my cook tent where it has grown smokey as your brother

C. W. Gamble.

Write to me soon, do!

Rappahannock River Bridge

Falmouth, Virginia.
February 3rd, 1863.

Dear Parents and Wife;-

I now take my pencil in hand to inform you that I received your letter this morning and was glad to hear from home once more and to hear that you were all enjoying good health. I for my own part am enjoying excellent good health, indeed, better than I have ever had since I have been in the army, as I think that cooking agrees with me better than to do army duty, as it seems to me more like work and it keeps me busy all of the time as I have about 70 men to cook for and have to cut off my own wood. The police carry my water for me and that takes off some of the hardest work.

At 5 o'clock every morning I am woke up by the guards and then I build my fire; by that time I get my water to make coffee, (about 8 gallons) some time I get it done before roll call and then I have to deal it out to them. Then I have to commence getting dinner and it keeps me busy all of the time as there is no one but myself. The other Companies have 2 cooks; but I generally have my meals ready by the time that they do.

But it is a hard thing for a man to cook for a Company, that is, to please every one. We have our days rations dealt out by the quarter master for each company and sometimes it is scant enough which makes a small quantity for each man and they growl at me for not giving them out more. I have to cut their meat they draw into 210 pieces so each man can have a piece three times in a day, and that is a good deal of work for me, and sometimes they get a very small piece and then they growl at me. Sometimes they get out of other rations and then some of them will growl; so a man has to have a great deal of patience to get along with all of them. But I get along the best that I can but it causes me often to say hard words and that we must do to get along with some of them.

It is getting unhandy for wood here now. When we came where our camp is now it was full of pine timber but it is all cut off now and we have to carry our wood for one mile as there is no timber for a mile around us now. We don't know but what we may stay here all winter now as Burnside has left us and the army now is quiet. Hooker has now taken charge of this army and there may be a change pretty soon and may be not before spring. I am in hopes there will be a change soon as I am getting tired of this place. There has been some rain and snow here but it does not stay long with us. This morning about 6 o'clock it commenced to snow, and at ten o'clock it stopped and cleared away but it is very cold. The roads are getting a little better now but they have been so bad that the teams cold hardly get along.

I got a letter from Annie yesterday morning and she stated that they had sickness in the family and that she had very sore eyes; I wrote her answer to her letter yester day. She said that she would send me a box of knick-knacks if we were going to stay here two weeks. I would be pleased for her to send me a box if I thought that I could get it safe. Although several are getting them they say that they are broken open at Washington before they are sent on here; but if she does send one I shall endeavor to get it.

You wished to know about Sam being in the hospital; he is in there but he came up to see me yesterday and he appears to be right smart but he is a little hoarse yet. He caught a heavy cold and he had a fever with it but not a very severe one. The doctor attended him but he had to go down to the hospital to see him instead of the doctor's coming up here. So I told him he had better go down there and stay rather than be walking back and forward and catching more cold all of the time, and he had to lay on the ground in his tent and in the hospital he could lay on a bed and could be better taken care of. So he took my advice and went there and if he don't get more cold he will be all right in a day or two. He told me that he was used to first rate and they took good care of him and give him what he wanted to eat. Tell his Mother so that she will not feel worried about him.

If you can get any good envelopes I wish that you would send me some as I can not get any here. Excuse my paper for I brought it from Woodbury and Eliza's peaches stained it in my knapsack. No more at present. Good-bye

From your Son and Husband
C. W. Gamble.

Union General
Ambrose E. Burnside
(Pictured at right)

Division Commander
Army of the Potomac

Born 1824 Died 1881

Union General
Joseph Hooker
(Pictured at left)

Division Commander
Army of the Potomac

Born 1814 Died 1879

Falmouth, Virginia
February 13th, 1863

Dear Parents and Wife;-

I now take my pencil in hand to inform you that I received your kind and welcome letter and it found me in good health. I was washing my shirts by my cook fire and as I had to wash my shirts to day I got up by 3 o'clock and boiled my water before I got breakfast and afterwards done my washing. As it is a fine day I think that they will have a fine chance to dry; it rains here nearly every other day. I hope that these few lines will find you enjoying good health.

I do not know that I have much news to tell you at present but I will say something. I suppose that you know that we are now under the command of Hooker instead of Burnside so it is not worth while for me to say much about him; but I must say something in his behalf: since we have been under his command we fare better for he gives us more to eat and better. He has ordered us to have fresh bread four times a week with potatoes twice a week; and fresh meat twice a week; and all of these things we now get, besides onions once a week, and it pleases the boys very much. We have got a new commissary and that makes it better for us too and better for me to as he tends to his business better than the old one did; he helps me in dealing out the grub. Well I must stop now and put on some potatoes to boil for dinner or the boys will growl.

I will now commence again; we have had supper. 14th. I undertook to finish this letter last night but my eyes watered so that I had to quit writing and I will undertake to finish it. I have just received a letter from Annie and she and all the family are well with the exceptions of colds and she has started me a box which I expect to get soon as she seems to feel confident that I will receive it. I went down and saw our wagon master and he told me if I would give him an order he would get it for me when it came to the station.

We had an other funeral in our regiment yesterday in Co. F.; his name was William Lake from Woodbury. There are several more in the regiment that are sick. Dave is well and Sam has come out of the hospital and does not look much the worse for wear and he says that he feels well enough now, but he is not on duty as yet.

They are granting furloughs for our soldiers to come home for ten days now and if I get a chance to get one I will come home this spring. Joel Abbott has gone home and I suppose you have seen him before this time. I told him to tell you if you wanted to send me a box he would fetch it for me. I do not know when I shall get a furlough as but 2 are allowed to go out of a Co. at a time; but when I do get one Dave and I want to come home together. Dan Gaskill is about to get one to day and if he does succeed in getting it he may be home soon. No more at present, but write soon.

Good-bye
C. W. Gamble.

Falmouth, Virginia
February 23rd, 1863.

Dear Parents and Wife:-

I now take my pencil in hand to inform you that I received your letter to day and it found me in good health and I was glad to hear that you was all well. I am still in my business cooking yet but have not cooked anything for two days as the weather has been so stormy; it has snowed here one day and night and it commenced on the 21st and stopped last night about seven o'clock, and the snow here now is about ten inches deep, and to day it is a clear day but the snow does not go very fast, as it is cold here now. I always thought that Virginia was a warm state but it is as cold here to day as I ever knew it to be in Jersey; and last night was a cold night but I slept right warm in my bunk, but some of the boys complained of the cold right hard; they not having but one blanket. I have got two blankets and I had one of them doubled, and the other single and my tent over me and my coat and my bed tick under me and with it kept right warm.

This morning I had to get up early to give out the grub to the pickets; they detailed twenty-eight men out of a company to go to day and they have got to stay till to morrow morning, and a cold night they will have of it, as they dare not have any fire as they are guarding along the Rappahannock, on this side and the rebels are on the other and they can holler to one another and do it when their officers are not about.

Dave has gone out as one of them. Henry has just gone over to the quartermasters to guard there, and he says he would rather be at home at Hiram Strang's than be here now. We have not drawn any pay yet and don't know when we shall so there is a great many would like to come home if they only had the money and that is the case with Dave Smith or he would have been home before this time.

I had an old friend to tell me if I wanted to come home he would let me have the money and he offered me a $20 dollar bill to come with but I believe I will not come till I get my pay for it is such a difficult matter to get through Washington now.

Mr. Abbott has not got back yet and they say they have got him arrested in Washington; and I have not received my box yet. I have sent to the depot three times and they say it haint there, and I don't think that I shall get it.

That machine I don't care about selling it; I may want to use it again. I would like for you to get them castings out of Dave's shop and take care of them for me; they are under the drill bench; tell Charlie Smith and he will get them for you.

We now have to draw grub again; we now have plenty to eat, we have bread all the time now, potatoes and onions, but some of them gets frozen before they get here, and beef we get twice a week, and that feeds us very well at this present time.

Father, I would like to come home and see you all, but I do not know whether I shall get to come on now, but if I get the chance and get paid off, me and Dave are going to try to come this spring or summer if they don't stop the furloughs.

Well I am getting cold and I must stop writing, so good-bye

From your son
C. W. Gamble

P.S. I would like for you to send me some postage stamps as it is impossible for me to get them here. Write soon and don't forget it, So Good-bye C. W. Gamble.

Dear Brother and Sister;-

I take my pencil in hand to inform you that I am well and hope that these few lines may find you all the same. I must ask you to excuse me for not writing an answer to your letter before this time as I thought I would not write until I got that you said that you sent me; but I have not got it yet and I have sent to the station for it three times and they say that it has not come yet so I have almost give out getting it so I thought I would not delay writing any longer as I would like to inform you of the case and what is the reason it has not come I cannot tell. I suppose it has stopped at Washington as they tell me that they rob all the boxes there; but it may probably come yet and when it does I will write and let you know.

Well Annie I am in the cooking business yet but have not cooked anything for 3 days as the weather has been so bad here for some time; I deal it out to them in the raw state and they cook it in their tents. It snowed here on the 21st and 22nd all day and the snow is now about 10 inches deep and we cannot get wood to cook with as we have to carry it on our backs for one mile and that is a hard way to get it now in the snow.

The weather here is clear and cold now and the snow is not going very fast but we will have to try to get some wood before long or stop eating. It is very cold here nights and some of our boys have got but one blanket; I have got two and with them and my over coat and my tent I can keep right comfortable in my cook tent. I am in hopes that it will get warmer in camping days for it is hard for us here in cold weather. They take 22 pickets out of each Company once a week to guard along the Rappahannock and the officers will not let them build any fires; and that is exposing duty for our boys as they have to lay on the ground without fire one night and day.

44

Our boys are on one side of the river and the Rebels are on the other side.

They can see each other plain. Well I must now bring my letter to a close and write more the next time. So Good bye

From Your Brother
C. W. Gamble.

Write as soon as you get this letter and let me know how you all are. I got a letter from home and they were all well.

Confederate Camp outside of Culpeper, Virginia

Falmouth, Virginia
March 10th, 1863

Dear Parents and Wife;-

I now take my pencil in hand to inform you that I received your letter this morning and one from Annie, and they found me in good health and I hope that these few lines will find you all enjoying the same blessing; your letter was dated the 23rd.

I received the box that Annie sent me on the 4th of this month which she started on the 10th of last month; it had been so long on the road that very nearly everything had spoiled. The mince pies and cake and pickles and mangoes and sausage meat had all spoiled. The peppermint, butter, sugar, apples, paper, envelopes and pepper was all right and nice. There was a whole chicken, baked nice, that was all spoiled so that I did not even get a taste of it; nor did I get a taste of the pies nor the cakes; but the doughnuts were good. Dave and I ate them; and the butter and apples were good. I was sorry that they spoiled, but I could not help it. I sent three times to the station for it, but they said that there was none there. If it had been started two weeks later it would have come all right and I would have received it at the same time that I did. It came to Aqua Creek all right, but it lay there so long that the things were spoiled when the boxes were brought to the regiment.

They said that there was about 900 boxes for different regiments. There were several that got boxes in our regiment; but pretty nearly all of them were spoiled. They say that now is a good chance to send boxes for they send them right on to the regiment now. My box had not been opened I don't think but some had by the looks of them.

I have now quit cooking for it hurt my eyes; since I have quit my eyes are getting better. I was on picket the other day on the Rappahannock and could talk to the Rebs; but our officers would

46

not let us talk to them if they knew it. The Rebs would send papers across to us in little boats and we would send coffee back in exchange; as coffee was in great demand with them. They would helloa to us and tell us to send coffee. The morning that we came away they started a plug of tobacco across to me for some coffee, but I was relieved before it got across so the other picket got it I suppose. The Rebs tries to be friendly to us and they said that they wished that the war was over.

We had to stay one day and night, and I don't think that I ever suffered as much in my life from the cold as I did that night. We could not have any fire of any account as there was no wood to be got of any kind as they had burnt every thing up fences and all. About daylight we went down in a valley and we built a fire out of some cornstalks which done a little good to warm by. After the sun got up it was warmer and at noon we started for camp.

I have not thought much about coming home until now for 4 or 5 days and nights I have been thinking and dreaming about home all of the time; and was afraid that something had happened to some of you which made me feel worried about it until I received your letter. I asked the Lieutenant the other day about giving furloughs for to come home. He asked me when I wanted to go and I told him the time and he said there was so many that he was going to let them draw. If I draw one and get paid off I will come home and see you as I want to see my wife and boy and all of the rest of you.

We have a great many sick in the hospital now; we have 16 out of our Company. Dan Gaskill is sick and has gone to the hospital. We have one in our Company that we have to carry pig-a-back when he wants to go out. He has the rheumatism in his legs. Dave Smith is well and is now making soup for himself and it looks as if it might be good too. Good-bye,

From Your Son and Husband
C. W. Gamble.

Falmouth, Virginia
March 26th, 1863.

Dear Parents;-

I now take my pencil in hand to inform you that I received your kind and welcome letter on the 25th and it found me enjoying good health yet; but I do not know how long I may enjoy such good health, as there are a great many of our boys sick in the regiment now, and several of them have died.

We buried three day before yesterday and one of them was out of our Company; his name was John Gardiner from Turnertown, Camden County; he was a corporal of our Company. I helped dig his grave and help put him in his box: I laid his overcoat under his head and laid his blanket across the box and laid him in it and then I folded the blanket over him and nailed him up. We put him on a stretcher and four of us carried him to his grave with the band ahead playing the dead march and we behind them with the corpse, and the rest of the Company behind us; and I tell you it is a solemn affair to bury a soldier so far from his home and so far away from his parents and friends. But we expect that his parents will come on after him and take him home this morning.

We had another one out of our Company die in the hospital and his name was Thomas Johnson; he was a corporal of our Company and he leaves a wife and child to mourn the loss of him; he is from the same place that Gardiner is from. That makes three out of our Company in one week; and some two or three more of our Company we do not expect to live as they are just alive and that is all. The other young man that was buried was Andrew Hastings from Penn's Grove, Salem County.

You stated that Hiram Strang wished to know how Daniel Gaskil was getting; he is getting well, and he is so that he is walking about a little now in good weather, but he looks badly. Henry and Dave are both under the Doctor's hands yet, but not so far but what they are stepping about. I have a cough that bothers me some at night, but with that exception I am as well as can be expected through the hardships we have passed through and the kind of weather we have had; it rains here every other day. Last week I was on picket three times as there are so many sick and off of duty and we that are well have to go on duty for them which makes it hard for those of us who are able to go on duty.

Last week we drew whiskey; and when it was dealed out to us they say that there were not many temperance soldiers among us for they all took their drink. I took mine and I don't think that I ever took a drink of whiskey in my life that did me more good than that drink did at that time as I had just come off of picket duty. I do not know whether they expect to draw it all the time or not, but I believe if we had it in the regiment and they would let us use it right it would be a benefit to the regiment and there would not be as many sick as there are now.

If I should be taken sick here I should like to be taken home to be buried with the rest of my brothers and sisters if possible and not to lay here in Virginia soil; but if I get killed in a battle there is no knowing where my body may be left. Sam Green is well and has gone on picket to day, but he don't look as rugged as he did before he was sick.

We are about to move our camp and put up our small tents; and Dave and Henry and Sam and myself are going to put up one together. We have commenced it and have split and hewn our stuff out of pine logs and then carry it a mile on our backs. It will take some time before we can get out tent finished so that we can move into it.

You requested me to let you know whether I got the envelopes and paper and stamps that you sent. I got them and they were very acceptable to me as they can not be got here. Father I would love to see you all once more and we are drawing furloughs now; and if I draw a furlough and get my pay I will come home and see you as I want to see my wife and boy badly and dream about them often. No more at present. So good-bye.

From your Son C. W. Gamble.

Write once a week to me Father, if you can as I like to hear from home.

Embalming Surgeon at work on unidentified Soldiers body
Photo courtesy the Library of Congress

Falmouth, Virginia
March 28th, 1863.

Dear Brother and Sister;-

I take my pencil in hand to inform you that I received your letter dated March 23rd and it found me enjoying good health as can be expected considering the hardships of a soldier's life. I have had a bad cough which makes it disagreeable for me but I am in hopes that I may recover from it in a few days; I hope that these few lines will find you all well. I received a letter from home yesterday and it stated that they were all well.

We now have a great many sick in the regiment and we bury one nearly every day. We have 20 sick in our Company and have buried 4 within 9 days but none that you are acquainted with. We draw rations for only 64 men and only about 30 of them are able for duty and that makes it hard for us that are able for duty as we have theirs to do too. I have to go on picket three times in a week and that is one day and a night each time and have to march about 5 miles through mud and water rain and snow and I tell you that it is very exposing to a man's health. We picket in the Rappahannock opposite the city of Fredericksburg and the Rebs on the other side of the river and they can talk across to each other but the officers won't let us talk to them.

I dug a grave the other day for one of our brother soldiers the first grave that I ever dug and helped them put him in his coffin. I put his overcoat under his head and laid his blanket across his box and laid him in the box and spread it both ways over him; then I nailed the lid over him and I then helped to carry him on stretchers on our shoulders to the grave the band ahead playing the Death March and the Company behind us and I tell you that it is a solemn office to bury one so far away from his parents and friends; but we expect that his friends will come and take their bodies home as they have been doing it in the regimen, them that are able to do it. If I should be taken sick and die I do not want to lay down here in Virginia. I want to be taken home and buried with the rest of the family if it takes all that I am worth.

You wanted to know whether I belonged to the 9 months men or no; I belong to the 3 years men but hope that the war may be over before my time is out as I am tired of serving under Uncle Sam. We may stay here for some time yet and we may not stay here a week and we cannot tell anything about it for we are under marching orders and have been for months so we cannot tell anything about it. But I do expect we shall move from here as soon as the roads will permit us to travel them with our artillery and pontoons; as they think we may have to go in battle soon as the Rebs are shooting at our pickets and they have had some sharp fights along the lines, but our men always proved to much for them.

We have some of our Pittstown boys sick in our regiment but none in the hospital, but they are under the Doctors hands. Among them are Dave Smith; he has been sick for some time and he thinks that he will never see home again. I am in hopes that we may all live to get home to see our families again. We have been drawing furloughs again for 10 days and there has been some 3 or 4 out of our Company has been home and I laid out to get one and to go home the first of April but they will not grant them for longer than 3 days now and that is to short a time for me to go home on as it will take the whole time for me to go and come an so I shall not be able to come home this time but I would like to see my wife and boy and, in fact, all the rest. Give the children all a kiss and tell them I sent it to them. So no more at present; excuse spelling and writing as I have a poor chance here to write so good bye

From Your Brother
C. W. Gamble.

52

Falmouth, Virginia
April 5th, 1863.

Dear Parents and Wife;-

I now take my pencil in hand to inform you that I received your kind and welcome letter and was glad to hear from home and to hear that you were all well. Your letter found me sitting by my fire in our tent.

It is snowing hard and the snow is about 6 inches deep and it had liked to have catched us out of doors and no tents to go into, as they took our large tents from us yesterday at 6 o'clock and it was an early hour to turn a man out of doors as cold as it was yesterday morning; but I suppose that they thought that we were soldiers and it did not make any difference to us; as I think some thinks that a soldier can stand anything and so it don't make any difference to them. We had no tent to go in to so we had to go to work to finish it; and we had a sharp time of it as we had two brigade drills that day, one in the forenoon and one in the afternoon and it did not give us much time to work at out tent; but we did what we could and I went to work and put up the chimney and lucky we were to. We had just got moved in our tent when it commenced to snow and it snowed all night and it is snowing this morning; but we are in our tent keeping ourselves as contented and comfortable as can be expected down here in Virginia. Dave keeps about one thing yet. The doctor attends him yet but he is not in the hospital; he is here in the tent with me now and has just laid down on his bunk to rest himself. Henry and Sam are here with me but they are grunting a little yet.

I wrote a letter for Sam this week to his Mother and I expect that she has received it before this.

We have several inspections and reviews here, but I think we had one here the other day that tore the handle off of all we ever had. We were all called out in line as usual and then were ordered to set down on the ground and pull off our boots and shoes to see if we had clean feet or not. It was the doctor's orders I believe; the doctor is Richard Gilman's son from Salem County. He found fault with one of the boys and said that the dirt on his feet had been on ever since last spring and someone made the reply that it was from Salem County and the Doctor said that it was a pity to bring Salem County mud down in Virginia.

We have a camp in front of us called the pontoon corps; and they have got some 200 wagons besides the loads of plank. I suppose there is 100 of them. It seems to me that something is going to be done as soon as the weather and roads will permit. For my own part I don't care how soon as I am getting tired of this kind of soldiering and I want the thing settled one way or the other either by a compromise or by fighting. If we have got to do it by fighting I say go to work and do it and have it over with. I for my own part am willing to fight for the Constitution as long as I have a drop of blood in my veins, and the longer I am here the more I feel like it.

We have a great many deaths in our regiment, nearly one every day; we have lost another one this morning, and he is out of our Company and his name is William Parks from Philadelphia, he is a potato peddler and his native place is about Franklinville. Watson knows him; he told me that he traded horses with Watson once. We took one up this morning and are going to send him home. His name is John Johnson from Turner town in Camden County. Daniel Gaskill is getting well slowly but has not got well enough to go on duty yet; but they took him to the hospital again but in nice weather he is out and comes up to see us; he received his box that his wife sent him and it was all right and nothing spoiled in it so if you want to send me one send it right away as they will come now in 4 days if you do send one send it soon as we may move shortly.

That settlement of Dave Hitchner I don't think is right for the year the road went through the lot I paid him and he throwed off ten dollars and said that I might have it quarterly at $20 a year and I see that he has got me charged $25.00 and that is not right. He only wanted to throw off $5.00 but I told him that I did not think that would do so he told me that he would charge me but $20.00 and when we settled up to the 25th of March coming and I owed him on the settlement and I built a bent to his barn since so I don't think that I owe him half the amount; and I think that the year for 1861 is settled for and the settlement in my book wrote to that effect if I am not mistaken very much. I want it right and don't want any more and I don't want to wrong any one out of a cent if I know it; and don't want them to cheat me as I wish to deal honestly with every one and that is my motto. See him and see what he says and report to me in the next and if it is not right if I live to get home I will make it right.

If you send me a box Dave tells me to tell you to tell his wife to send him a box too. He has just woke up now and he is as cross as he can be. He is going to eat a boiled potato directly and that may fetch him in a good humor again. Give my respects to all inquiring friends. VanSant and Dave DuBois especially; and tell them I want them to send me answers to those letters that I sent them or if I get home I will not come and see them. Don't forget to tell them. So good bye from

Your Son and Husband
C. W. Gamble.

Dear Parents and Wife;-

I take my pencil in hand to inform you that I am well at present and hope that these few lines will find you all enjoying the same blessing.

Well we have moved and have been three days on the march and have got here at a place not more than a mile from the battle ground, and can hear the cannon, and did hear them last night for some time. We expect to have to be in battle before night and it may be the last letter that I may be permitted to write you, but I am in hopes it may not be the case; but if it is my lot I must go.

Sam got him letter and tobacco last night and was pleased with it and I read it for him and I saw that you had wrote a few lines to me. I wrote you a letter as soon as I received the box, but I suppose you did not get it until after you had written Sam's letter or you would have said something about it.

The report here is that Fredericksburg is in possession of our forces and they have taken it since we have been on the march from our camp at Falmouth, but how true it is I cannot say. We are having very bad weather here; it rains here every day, or it has rained every day since we have been on the march. The first day we marched until noon and then we ate dinner and I was detailed to go out and work on the Corduroy road; I had to take my knapsack and grub with me and they were a load for me; but when we got in line we had to take a spade or axe or pick which made our load still heavier

– all together I suppose about 70 lbs. to carry, and if I had been at home I could not have stood it, but I have stood it first rate yet, and don't feel the least sore.

Sam wanted me to write a letter for him but I haven't got the time so I will put a few words in here for him; he is well and is ready to go in battle he says at any time. Dave and I put up in our tent together, and he is writing a letter home too, so it is not worth while for me to say much about him. I want you to write to me as soon as you receive this letter. The mail boy follows us all the time now. No more at present, but remain

Your Son and Husband
C. W. Gamble.

Falmouth, Virginia.
April 26th, 1863

Dear Parents and Wife;-

I now take my pen in hand to inform you that I am well with the exception of my eyes and they are quite sore yet. I have got cold in them and they run with water all the time which makes it quite unpleasant to me especially when the sun shines.

Well, Father we have got the box that you sent to us; we got it last night and Dave and myself were pleased to get it. Everything was all right except the eggs and they were spoiled as we could not eat them; the box came to the station all in time and it was sent to Head-Quarters and there it laid till yesterday when they were sent in to us. I think every thing you sent to us arrived here safe as the box leaked as if it had not been disturbed. We were uneasy about the box for fear we would not get it as we had orders to get eight days rations and get ready to move the next day after you started the box. I went down to the station to see about the box and they told me they had sent all the boxes to the regiments, but if we had moved we would not have got the box until everything had spoiled; and we should have been very sorry about it after you had taken so much pains to try to send us one. We gave Sam all of his things and gave him some of our knick-knacks as you call them, and he was pleased with his tobacco for he was starving to death for the want of tobacco.

George was over to see us yesterday and he is fat and hearty as a bird, and is the same George. He gave us some tobacco and that pleased us much, and he bought us a paper as we had no money and he had as he had been paid off about a week ago. We have not been paid yet; we have got six months pay coming to us now but cannot tell when we shall get it but the papers say that we shall be paid off soon and it will take about $5,000,000 to do it.

We have not moved yet but do expect to go every day as we have to keep eight days rations in our knapsacks and haversacks. We have sent part of our clothes ahead so as to give room to carry our grub and we shall have as much as we shall want to carry on a march and we cannot tell where we shall go to yet but when we do move I will write to you if I am alive and let you know where we are.

I was over in Fredericksburg the other day I helped row a boat across with a flag of truce with one of Hooker's staff officers; he had a dispatch for them and I heard all they had to say to each other; they talked very friendly to each other and exchanged papers and letters. When we arrived on the other side we did not see many Rebs but they raised out of their rifle pits like bees when we landed, and a hard looking set they were. They had no uniform on their clothes were dirty and ragged, but the officers were dressed in uniform, and looked as nice as our officers.

We live in our tent quite comfortable now; there are five of us in it, and we cook for ourselves. I do the cooking and the rest set the table and wash the dishes and carry water; when I am on duty Dave does the cooking or some one of the rest.

Tell Lib Smith that we got the box and it was all right except the eggs and they were spoiled. Tell Bess Watson that I got the paper and tobacco, and it was all right and I will write to Mr. Watson as soon as convenient. No more so good-bye.

From Your Son and Husband
C. W. Gamble

Camp on the Battlefield
May 2nd, 1863

Dear Parents and Wife;-

I now take my pencil in hand to inform you that I am well with the exception of sore eyes, and am in hopes these few lines will find you all in good health.

Well we are now as you might say in the battle; they are banging away at the Rebs as hard as they can and we are laying back on reserve, but to go in shortly as it does not come our turn next; I may be cut down before you receive this letter. We are within 3-4 mile of where they are now fighting; we have had orders to go now immediately, no more this time; ---

May 3rd. We marched down in front of the Rebs under the fire of shells last night and some bursted in our regiment and wounded some of our men, but we did not get into battle until morning. At day break we were ordered in line and laid down on our stomachs and waited for the enemy. At last they came and we commenced firing on them. Our colonel was wounded the first round and then we had no commander and the regiment wandered everywhere; at last our lieutenant took command and we commenced firing. The balls struck all around me, John White, Enos Garrison, Harrison Johnson, Joel Abbott were all wounded along side of me, but I was spared. I was hit with one spent ball below the knee and the ball fell about four feet from me and I got the ball. I got out without getting hurt.

We got out in the field; they commenced shelling us and a shell struck near me and wounded several and a piece went through my knapsack and blanket while I was in it with my knees, but did not hurt me. We had to retreat back out of the field; we have got several wounded in our regiment and several killed. Dave Smith was hit on

60

the shoulder with a ball which left quite a mark. We went back in the woods and there we laid all day, but we are on the battle field yet and they are fighting around us all the time; and we are staying here waiting for an attack and expect to be in every minute, if we only had our colonel I would not be in the least afraid, but we have not got him to command us and I am afraid that we shall fare badly. But we shall have to do the best that we can; one thing we can say we have got a good Lieutenant and I shall put my trust in him and the God above us all. No more at present but I remain

Your Son and Husband,
C. W. Gamble.

The Battle of Chancellorsville
April 30-May 6, 1863

Print by Kurz and Allison

Depicts the wounding of Confederate Lt. Gen. Stonewall Jackson
on May 2, 1863

61

Dear Parents and Wife;-

I take my pencil in hand to inform you that I received your letter yesterday and was glad to hear that you were all well. I was corporal of the guard at the brigade quarters when my letter came and Dave, knowing that I wanted to hear from home so badly, brought it over to me and I read it with such pleasure. When I saw that it was not Fathers writing I was afraid that he was sick but I soon found that he was all right and that it was from Annie; and she stated that you were all well I then felt myself satisfied.

I had been looking for a letter for some time as I had written three letters home since the battle and had not received any answer but one, and that was but a few lines. I had no postage stamps to put on the two last ones and maybe that was the reason they did not come. We cannot get postage stamps here for love or money and if you can get them there I would like for you to send me some if you please.

You stated in your letter that you had got my picture and that Annie said that it did not look like me (or not like I used to look) and none of the rest said anything about it; not even Eliza and I would like to know whether any of the rest of you had seen it or not; if you have seen it I would like to know what you think about it, and how my wife Eliza is getting along and what she is doing and whether she has enough to eat or not. You say that she and George are well and that is about all I can hear about them. I want to know whether she lives in Pittstown or not, and whether she has got any garden or not, and if she has I want to know how it looks. I sent her a ring that I made out of a bone in Virginia and I made it just to pass away the time.

I would like to get home on a furlough and had a prospect of doing it and did expect to be there this month, but they have stopped granting furloughs again. So I cannot tell whether I shall get home this summer or not.

We are under marching orders again and expect to go every day and have got everything packed up for to start and the teams are standing around the camp ready to load up any minute; and we have got three days rations cooked for a start and we expect that we shall be in another hard battle before the week is out as our forces have commenced firing below Fredericksburg night before last about 5 o'clock and there was some heavy cannonadeing I tell you. They say that we have got two pontoon bridges across the Rappahannock and that our forces have crossed and that our flag waves over the town of Fredericksburg; but I cannot tell you whether it is so or not for we don't know anything what is going on here within three mile of us; as we are not allowed to go out of the lines of our brigade; if we do we have to be court-marshalled. It has not been tried on me as yet but I have seen others court-marshalled and it don't look very pleasant. We have someone in the regiment court-marshalled every day and sometimes three or four of a day.

We have to go out on drill at half past five o'clock in the morning and that is before a great many has breakfast; but Dave and myself generally has breakfast before we go out on drill. Them that don't go out on drill has to be court-marshalled; and we have to go out at 6 o'clock in the afternoon on drill till dark and then we have to get our supper. After we have got that we go to sleep. Between time we do police duty and keep our guns and clothes clean; that takes all of our time very nearly, so you may know what time we have to spare. It is not worthwhile for me to tell you anything about the war or battles for you know sooner and more about it than we do here. They are taking the sick out of the regiment to the hospital this morning and that indicates that we shall be in battle soon. Our officers say we are laying back as reserve and when we do go in battle we will have to fight like soldiers for the reserves have the hardest fighting to do when they do go in. If we do have to go in battle I hope that I may get out safe again as I did in the first one all though I escaped some pretty close shaves, for I would like to see you all once more. Dave is well and is here in the tent with me now while the rest are gone out to drill, but he says that he must put some beans on to cook.

Dan Gaskill is in the hospital yet; but he walked over here the other day and he stayed all night with us. He looks better than I ever saw him look and he says that he feels better and weighs more. He intended to come back to the camp but he has not come in account of the move.

Write as soon as you get this letter and tell me all about the times. No more at present, but good-bye. I remain

Your Son and Husband
C. W. Gamble.

Ruins of Houses in Fredericksburg, Virginia
Photo courtesy of the Library of Congress

On the March in Virginia
Near the Orange and Ohio
Rail-road, June 18th, '63

Dear Parents and Wife;-

I now take my pencil in hand to inform you that I am on the land and among the living, and enjoying as good health as can be expected, being on a force march and as warm and dry as it is in Virginia. This is the first force march we have had and I tell you, it is a hard march for us this hot weather; it keeps all the doctors busy to keep the men from dying all along the road. We have lost some five or six men from heat and have had several killed by the Rebel Bush-whackers; but I have stood it very well.

We have been marching three days and one night and a good many of the boys have got nothing but a gum blanket and a haversack, having thrown everything else away. Dave and I stick to our knapsacks yet and clothes and tent and blanket.

They say that we are going in to Pennsylvania, but how true it is I cannot say, but I hope that it is so, for I think that I can fight better at home than I can in Virginia. They say that we are going to take a days rest and then we are going on until we come to the battle ground. We have got a Cavalry back of us a burning everything that they can on the road and I think that we will have a tight time for a few weeks, but I still hope that I may live through it. We are now in the pine woods and the pines are so thick that you can not see a man a hundred yards away from you and it is almost as hot in here as it is in an oven, and Dave and I are laying on our stomachs writing letters home. I have not received but one letter from you since the battle of Chancellor's Ville. (I received the letter than Annie sent me) but none from you, and am quite uneasy about you all at home, thinking that there is something the matter and you don't want to let me know it; but I will still keep on writing and maybe I will get an answer from some one of them.

We live on raw pork and hard tack on this march and coffee when we have a chance to make it. We have forded a great many streams and always stop by one when we stop for the night, which gives us a chance to go in and wash our selves. We marched through a town called Dumphries and after we left the Rebs shot some of our men that were behind and the Cavalry burnt several of the houses in there. If I live and get in Pennsylvania I may stand a chance to get home for a few days, but I am afraid that will not be the case.

Father, I want you to write to me as often as you can make it convenient to do so, as I want to hear from home; don't wait for me to write for we have a poor chance to write letters on the march; direct them to Washington to follow the regiment. I will now bring my letter to a close by saying good bye to you all.

From Your Son,
C. W. Gamble.

Gainesville, Virginia
June 25th, 1863

Dear Parents and Wife;-

I take my pencil in hand to inform you that I am well at present and hope these few lines may find you all enjoying the same blessing.

I have now been chosen by our major for a corporal of our Company, and wear the stripes as such; I am on duty to day with 12 guards on the Alexander & Mt Jackson R.R., and I have had a good mess of red heart cherries this morning. They are the first fruit that I have had since I have been in Virginia.

We are between two villages; one called Gainesville and the other Haymarket. You can see it on the map of Virginia. The village called Haymarket has been burnt down; there is a church left in the village and that is all the building that has escaped the flames. It looks as if it has been a nice village at one time.

We were on the march five days and one night; and a force march at that. There were several that died on the road. We marched through a town called Dumphries and a town called Centerville and through Bull Run battle ground; there I saw a sad sight, one that I never had seen before; it was dead soldiers buried or undertaken to be, but they had only had dirt thrown over them, and some of their hands and arms were sticking out with the flesh all off of them; and some with their heads sticking out, some with one leg and foot with a shoe on. I tell you it was a sad sight for me to look at and a hard one to think of. We could see through the woods that we passed through trees that had been cut off by shells as large as eight inches through and trees that had been struck by balls all through the woods, all showing that there had been a hard fight.

All the troops have left us but our division, and that is Frenche's Division. We are encamped in a field back of the village of

67

Gainesville where we are saved as a reserve and don't know how soon we may have to move from here.

There were two trains of cars came in on the road on the 23rd loaded with grub and forage and I was one of the details to help unload them; there was ten car loads on each train. They say that there has not been a train on the road for a year.

The relief has come and I must stop.   I am relieved now for to day, I being a Corporal it makes my duties easier.   The cars have just come in but have gone out again and word has come that we are packed up in camp and are going away from here to day, but how true it is I can't say.

I saw some nice farms on our march; one at Centerville that I took particular notice of, and that had been a nice one but the country around here looks about the same as in other parts of the state that I have been in: that is, hilly and stony.

We have just got a newspaper the first one we have had since leaving Falmouth, but what the news is I can not tell as I am busy writing and can not listen to it, but I suppose you know more about the news than we do. No more at present but remain

Your son and husband
C. W. Gamble

Dear Parents and Wife;-

I now take my pencil in hand to inform you that I am well and on the land and among the living, and hope these few lines my find you the same.

I have been in a hard battle fought at a place called Gettysburg, and an awful battle it was I tell you. The hardest fight was on the 3rd of this month and our brigade being in front of the engagement we had the fighting to do. I laid under an apple tree under the fire of the shells for thirty minutes and there was one fired every second and I expected every moment might be my last, for I expected to be struck with one of the shells, as they were killing all around me, cutting off limbs of trees and killing horses. At last a piece of shell struck me on the foot which made it sting very sharp bruising my toe, but not seriously. Our company laid about 50 yards from me behind a stone fence. At last they stopped shelling and I saw three lines of Rebs start out to charge on us, so I got up and went to my company; we waited until they got in reach of us and then we opened fire on them, and we cut them down like wheat. At last the white handkerchiefs commenced flying as flags of truce, and we took about two or three thousand prisoners and seventeen flags. The field laid thick with killed and wounded and an awful sight it was to me. I tell you the old 12th showed its bravery here and our Generals gave us the praise and said they were not afraid of the Jersey Boys now.

The night before the battle three Companies of our Regiment made a charge of bayonets on a barn where several Rebs were quartered; several of the boys were wounded and some killed, but the rest went on and took about 150 prisoners and brought them in the regiment. The next night we made another charge but did not get many prisoners and some of the boys got wounded; among them were

Enos Garrison and Samuel Green wounded in the arm not very badly, but they had to go to the hospital; Isaac DuBois was wounded too, and he is in the hospital also. We have had 5 wounded in our Company and none killed. Our Lieutenant was hit with a ball in the hip but not so as to take him off duty.

Yesterday we were all day burying the dead Rebs, supposed to be over two thousand and about two hundred in front of our Company; and an awful job it was; some with their guts hanging out, and some with their brains out and legs and arms mashed off, but we buried them all and left the battle field; and we are going to be relieved and when we get settled down I will give you the whole details of the battle. So no more; write to me soon; Good-bye

From Your Son
C. W. Gamble.

Read this letter to Lize. The same day I got a letter from her. Direct your letters as before.

Breastworks on Little Round Top Gettysburg, Pa., 1863

Gettysburg, Pennsylvania.
Three Confederate
Prisoners.

Photo by:
Mathew Brady

Gettysburg, Pa. Interior view of breastworks on extreme left of the Federal line. This 1863 photograph shows the extreme advantage of the Union troops at Gettysburg. This photo shows an ideal defensive position on the left of the Federal lines. You can see that they occupy the "high ground" with significant boulders to protect their position.

On the March Again;
Near a Town Called the Two Taverns
On the Baltimore Turnpike, Pa.
July 6th, 1863

My Dear Wife;-

I now take my pencil in hand to inform you that I am well, and I hope that these few lines will find you the same. I received a letter from you to day, dated June 29th, and one from Father, dated 24th, and they found me on the land and among the living.

We have been on the march for three weeks and have been in a battle and a hard one it was too. It commenced on the first and lasted till the third and we being in the front, we had the hardest fighting to do. Our regiment was ordered to charge bayonets on a barn and it was full of Rebs, and we did it and they fired at us pretty sharp and wounded several of our regiment; but we took the barn and 150 prisoners with it. Among the wounded was Sam Green; he was hit in the arm, so he has to be in the hospital. Enos Garrison and Isaac DuBois were also wounded and they are in the hospital too.

On the third our batteries opened on the enemy and it lasted about 30 minutes, and there was a cannon fired every second during that time. I laid under an apple tree about 50 yards from the company when it commenced and I could not get to it until the cannon stopped firing; the shells and balls fell all around me; cutting limbs off of the trees by me; at last a piece of shell hit my foot and bruised one of my toes pretty bad. As soon as the cannons stopped firing the Rebels charged on us; as soon as I saw them get out in line I went into my company. When they got within firing distance we commenced and we cut them down like wheat; we killed over 200 right in front of our company and took 17 flags and over 2000 prisoners, and we only had one man wounded in our company as we were behind a stone fence.

There was over 2,000 killed and wounded laid on the field and an awful sight it was too, and to hear the cries of the wounded. The killed and wounded Rebels laid on the field until the 5th, as the Rebel sharp-shooters fired on us when ever we endeavored to take them off, and it rained nearly all the time.

Yesterday we took the wounded Rebels to the hospital and buried the dead ones, numbering about 2,000, and an awful job it was too. I thought that I could not stand it, but I am getting so I think that I can stand most anything. Some of them had there entrails hanging out; some with their brains out; some with their heads one half off and gone; some their legs torn all to pieces. We dug a trench and buried 25 or 30 in one grave and had to drag them to their graves and they smelt bad I tell you.

After we got them buried we started off of the battle field about three o'clock and marched here by about 11 o'clock where we are now. They say that we have been relieved from the front and we are going to encamp to get recruited up and they say that we are going near Baltimore, but how true it is I can not say, but I hope it may be the case, as I am getting tired of marching; we do expect to start away from here any minute.

I have done as hard fighting as any one in the regiment, and I guess that I have fired as many rounds and have not been hurt seriously yet but the next battle I may be shot down the first one, and if it is my lot I will feel that I will die in a good cause; and if we should not see each other again in this world I hope that we may meet again in the other.

I was glad to get a letter from your heart and it done me good to read it, and to hear that you were getting along so well, and that George had got pants on. I would like to see you all, but I can not tell when it will be.
News has just come in that Lee has lost 40,000 men and that General French has had to burn his pontoon bridges, so I think that his army is very nearly crippled up, and Longstreet is dead.

Eliza, please send me some envelopes as I can get none here. Tell Dave I have not received any letters from him as yet. I will send you a $10.00 bill in Confederate money; you can show it to my friends; it is not worth any thing but it may be a sight to see it: it was taken out of the dead Rebels pockets, our boys have got several of them. Some have as high as $50.00 or $60.00 in gold: but I never disturb their pockets. No more at present.

Good-bye
C. W. Gamble.

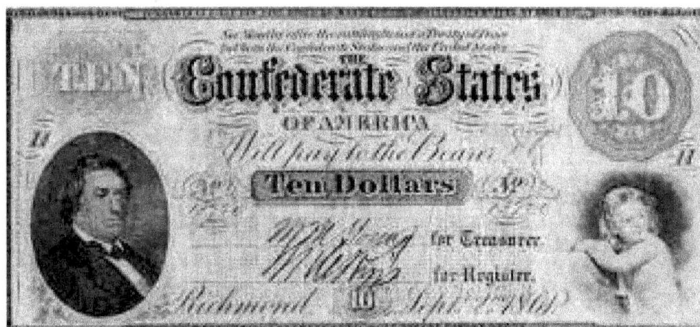

Antietam Battle Ground
Maryland, July 11, '63

Dear Parents and Wife;-

I now take my pencil in hand to inform you that I received a letter from you yesterday dated the 5th, and was glad to hear that you were all well' your letter found me enjoying the same with the exception of my feet; and they are very nearly worn out; as we have been chasing the Rebs through Pennsylvania and Maryland for four weeks. When we overtake them we commence battle with them. We had some hard battles with them at Gettysburg which I stated in my letters if you have got them; I sent two, one to my wife and one to you. I see in your letter that you have not gotten them.

We are on the ground where they had a small fight yesterday morning, and we expected to be in battle before this time; but I was out on picket last night with a squad of men and we heard no signs of them. But I think that they must be within 20 miles of us now, but I may be mistaken; they may be close to hand, if they are our General will find them and then we may have to give them battle. He is a brave and bold General; his name is Mead.

We have been in front of battle all the time. When we started from Woodbury we numbered 984 men; now we only draw grub for 425 in the whole regiment. So you can see it is getting quite small and if it keeps on the way it has been going in the course of two years we will not have a man in the regiment. At 10 o'clock we are laying along the road waiting for orders; they say the Rebs are within two miles of us trying to get across into Virginia. I think that they will have a tight time if they get back. The Rebs are falling back and coming in to our lines every day, and they have to keep out pickets in the rear to keep them in ranks. Some thinks if we keep on defeating them as we have been doing the fighting will soon be over and I hope it will, as I would like to see home once more and have the pleasure of telling you all about the war.

In the letter I sent a $10.00 bill of the confederate money, so that you can see what kind of money they have; I got it from one of our boys as rejoice to pick the dead Rebs pockets. I carried several of them water and so did the rest of the boys. We had one boy, William Riggins, got a $20.00 gold piece and a 2 ½ gold piece out of one of their pockets; you could see the boys all over the field. A lady has just told me the name of the place that we are in; she says it is Stillmentown and it is about the size of Pittstown.

I wrote for Eliza to send me some envelopes and stamps if she could as I have got mine all spoiled on the march, and I cannot get them here. You stated in your letter that I had not said anything about Dave Smith. The reason I did not he wrote home at the same time he is well. Sam Green is in the hospital yet wounded in the arm. Dan Gaskill is well when I last saw him but I don't know where he is now. Don't forget to write soon. Ask Eliza if she has got that ring yet I think I sent in G. Watson's letter. No more at present. Good bye all,

From Your Son
C. W. Gamble.

General George Meade

Defeated Confederate General Robert E. Lee at the Battle of Gettysburg

Born December 31, 1815
Died November 6, 1872

Harper's Ferry, Maryland.
July 17th, 1863.

Dear Parents and Wife;-

I now take my pencil in hand to inform you that I am well at present and hope that these few lines may find you all the same. We are encamped on a mountain called Maryland Heights; and we expect to stay here two or three days. Where we are going to then I can not tell. I suppose that we are laying here to get rested as we have been on the march for five weeks and have been in one hard battle (that was the battle of Gettysburg). Since that we have been chasing up the old fox (Lee) trying to catch him but he got away from us and crossed the Potomac into Virginia again; but we captured a large number of prisoners and part of his train of wagons and a large quantity of arms. But he escaped and I think that he is one of the greatest generals and the smartest in the Rebel army. I think that if we had defeated him the war would have soon been over.

Since we have been on the march we have passed through a great many towns and seen other sights; we have marched through the State of Pennsylvania and all through the State of Maryland. I have stood it very well with the exception of my feet and the bottom of them get very sore as we had some very rough roads to travel and some large streams to ford. Dave stood it very well; better than I expected for he has been on the grunt pretty much all of the time and we had some very hard marching to do. We marched from 15 to 35 miles in a day, and they hardly gave us time enough to make our coffee. We are both of us getting very thin around the waist.

After we passed through Fredrick they took us through the fields to show us the Rebel Spy that General French had hung the day before; we saw him and it was one of the awfulest sights I ever saw in my life. He was stark naked and was yet hanging there and the hot sun had drawn blisters all over him. They said that his son had to come there at 9 o'clock and cut him down and take his place.

77

We marched within a mile of the Rebs and at night we went to throwing up an entrenchment about two miles long. We expected the Rebs to attack us in the morning but they did not come, so we advanced towards them for about a half a mile, where we stayed all night. In the morning we advanced up to their entrenchments and they had left during the night and had crossed the Potomac, but had left part of the army on this side which we took prisoners. Then we stayed there all night and in the morning we started for this place. We struck the canal at the mouth of Antietam Creek and then we marched up the tow path along the canal to Harper's Ferry and we stayed there for the night.

In the morning we marched to this place where we are now in camp. We are now drawing some clothes as some of the boys are nearly naked and no shoes on their feet. I had to wear my shirt for four weeks and it had liked to have grown fast to me as I had no time to wash it. At last I had time to wash it but it took me 2 days to get it dry, as it rains here every other day and is raining now while I am writing this letter. Dave is setting along side of me mending his haversack and sewing on his buttons and has been all morning and he says that he is not done yet. We are all getting lousey and one has to scratch the other as it is too much work for one to do.

Dave went down to the Doctor's this morning and he says that he has got about a pint of oil in him and he reckons that it will kick up a great running time directly. Our orderly has built a fire before our tent and that kicks up a great smoke and that comes into our tent and we are both quite ill-natured about it; but we must have something to bother us as it would not do to live to comfortable here for if the officers should find it out they would have us out of here pretty quick.

I think that we will leave here to-morrow but where we are going I cannot tell; but I think that we are going across the Potomac in Virginia again as we have got the Rebs out of Pennsylvania and Maryland. If we do cross the Potomac I shall hate it as I do not

78

want to step my foot on Virginia soil any more as I am tired of being in the State and don't want to go over there any more. I don't feel like fighting them in Virginia, but if they will come into Maryland or Pennsylvania I can fight them with more encouragement for it seems like fighting for our own State.

Where the Rebs have traveled in the States of Maryland and Pennsylvania they have destroyed a great deal of property and stock. In some places they have stripped the farmers of everything there was. One place in particular where there lived a widow close by the entrenchments; they took her horses and cattle, hogs, sheep, and all of her pork and hams out of her cellar and all of the flour and destroyed her garden and even destroyed her bees, every hive that she had and they destroyed her clothes about the house and ramsacked it all over and took anything that they liked. I tell you I think if we had been there about that time we would have give them the devil! as we Jersey Boys cannot stand that.

Father and Wife I do not know whether I ever shall see you any more and I would like for you to write to me as often as you can manage to do. Direct as before. Read this letter to my Wife and all the rest that I send you, if you please as I have left her in your care a while I am gone. No more at present so Good-bye

From Your Son and Husband
C. W. Gamble.

WRITE SOON.

Dear Wife and Parents;-

I now take my pencil in hand to inform you that I am well at present and I hope that these few lines will find you all the same. I wrote you a letter yesterday stating that I thought that we would move this morning and it is the case; we have moved and got in Virginia again. We came back to Harper's Ferry and crossed the Potomac on a Pontoon Bridge and then we crossed the Shenandoah River on a wire bridge, and then we marched about 1 mile and then we stopped to rest; I thought that I must write to you to let you know where I was.

I received three letters yesterday after I had written one to you. 1 from my wife; and 1 from Father; and 1 from my sister Rachel; it being the first that I have received from her and it was dated the 5th of June. It stated that they were all well excepting herself and she had the rheumatism in her arms. They were all very welcome for I do delight to hear from you all.

Yesterday our Lieutenant was promoted to Captin of our Company and our 2nd Lieutenant was promoted to first Lieutenant and I was appointed Commissary of the Company to fill the place of our Commissary that was wounded in our last battle. It clears me from all guard and picket duty as I am the first Corporal of the Company. They give us one hour to cook our coffee for diner and have not got much time to write but I thought that I must write something to let you know that I received your letters and paper, envelopes and stamps.

We are on the march again and where we are going I can not tell but I think that we are going to Winchester and that is about 60 miles from here; and it may be that we will be in battle before we get

80

there, as they had a sharp battle on the road day before yesterday and we may run a foul of them same ones. If they show fight we are the boys that never backs out but will fight to the death. I began to think that it is no more for us to go in a fight than it is to go hunting.

You stated in your letter that you would like to know where Isaac DuBois was wounded; I think that he was wounded in the leg or ankle; When he came out of the battle he passed by me, and said to me with a smile "Charlie, they gave it to me this time: and I asked him where and I think that he told me in the leg. He could walk on it and I think that he walked to the hospital. Enos Garrison is in a Hospital in Newark, New Jersey and I think that the rest of the boys are there as each state has to take care of their wounded.

Dave is with me now on the march and you stated in your letter that Lib Smith wanted to know what was the reason that he did not write. He says that when he stops to rest he wants to rest and is too tired to write. He has no encouragement to write an answer to the letters that she sends him, for she is all the time finding fault with him and complaining of him and wanting to put the children out to work, supposing his income is not large enough to maintain them. I, for my part, think that Dave does the best that he knows, for he sends her nearly all of the money that he gets and can spare for we must have some to get along with here. I have read some of her letters and I know what they are myself. I think that we are in a good cause and show that we are for our Country and Constitution, and I think if she is a good union woman she ought to encourage him. When he sent her some money she found fault with that and said that he had ought to have sent more. I know that he sent the same that I did and I sent $30.00 and he sent the same amount and had sent her $10.00 before that.

She found fault with his likeness and said that he looked as if he was drunk and believed that he was; as for that part I know that was not the case for him and myself worked hard to get them taken so we could send them home to our friends thinking that she would be glad to see them and she found fault and to send such an answer back to him as if she cared more about his money than she cared

81

about him. If I had got such an answer as he did I should have thought the same thing of you and would have thought that you had some other man there that you cared more about than you did me, I, being in the army and a far distance from you; but that was not the case with you and I trust in God that it may not be the case.

I for my part endeavor to send every cent of money that I can spare and you appear to be well satisfied with it. I always want to keep enough money on hand to fetch me home if I should get a furlough and that is the case with him; and we must have some to get tobacco with and some time some butter and other things that we don't have, and we have to pay a big price for them. Since we have been on the march we have been short of rations and those that had money could go out to the farm houses and buy bread and pies and we had to pay a big price for them. But we must have something to eat and could not go without. I hope that she will send letters to encourage him in his cause and not to discourage him for his sickness is bad enough. I don't --------(unreadable) as a slur to her as she might call it but for her own good and his too and he is sitting along side of me while I am writing it and he has read all of it.

We are now about on the march and I must bring my letter to a close. By saying Good-bye

From Your Son and Husband
C. W. Gamble.

N.B.!!! Take this to Elizabeth Smith and let her read it if she can, but she must excuse the writing and spelling for I can not do either one. C.W.G.

Camp Near Warrenton
Junction, Virginia
July 29th, 1863.

Dear Wife and Parents;-

I now take my pencil in hand to inform you that I received your welcome letter and the postage stamps and it found me in good health and I hope that this letter may find you all the same. We have been here two days and I hope that we will stay here a week so that we may get rested as we have been on the march for 43 days and a hard march; and you must judge that we want some rest by this time. They say that it is the hardest march that was ever done in this country by any army; I hope that the hardest part of our Campaign is over for the Summer. I think that we have had some of the hottest days here that I ever did experience in my life. Although it rains here very nearly every other day and night.

We are now where we can get plenty of rations again but we have been scant of them for some time and we could not have got along without starving if we had not went on foraging expeditions. Our boys would go out and fetch in fresh pork, mutton and veal; chickens, potatoes and green beans and we made out very well. Dave and myself have not done any foraging yet but we had some one to do it for us; for we have not got a heart large enough to go to so many houses and kill hogs and sheep and take chickens from the women. But we have enough that like to do such work and it is no hardship for them to do it.

Day before yesterday there was three companies of us detailed to guard the wagon train; and when we stopped at night the boys killed 2 hogs and skinned them and we had fresh pork for breakfast. Dave and I each had a slice of liver for breakfast too; while we were there a Lieutenant in another regiment gave us a calf and we went to work and killed that and Dave and I helped butcher that so we have had plenty of meat. Our train of wagons has all got loaded up again and we have got plenty of grub on hand now. Yesterday I drew whiskey for our boys and a pesky set they were; I drew full rations for them again and pickles and pickled onions and I tell you that they were sour and they were good too, and they were a great rarity for us.

We have had plenty of blackberries since we have been on the march as they are very thick in this part of Virginia and they are as large as your thumb; we picked them and put them in our cups and put sugar on them and a fine dish it makes too I tell you, but the great object is to get the sugar as we have not drawn any for some time back, but now we have plenty of it and the boys are enjoying them selves with it and they all appear to be in good spirits this morning for they all have got plenty of grub on hand now. When grub gets short the boys are in low spirits I tell you and when the quarter master happens to pass through the camp you ought to hear them yell "hard-tack" and he soon knows that the boys are out of hardtack and he will endeavor to get some for them as he is a fine man and looks to us boys interests; and says that we shall not want for grub if it is to be got for us.

I want to tell Dave DuBois I have not received any letter from him yet; and you stated in your letter that he had sent me two of them but I have never got them and tell him to write again and when we get into camp for to stay I will write a letter to him telling him all about the war if it takes a quire of paper.

I think that our campaign is very nearly over for this summer. We are now going to have our regiment filled up with the companies from Jersey and have sent 10 men out of the regiment after them. It takes over 400 men to fill up our regiment and we want to get our number out of Jersey if we can get them we expect to be filled up within 30 days. When we get them I expect we will have a sharp time of drilling them. If any of the boys are to be drafted around there that we know tell them to come in our regiment and we will make soldiers out of them.

I must tell you of a circumstance that happened the other day on the march with Captain Thompson of our regiment and an officer in the

12 corps wagon train. Our regiment was guarding our train and Captain Thompson was Captain of it and our train or wagons was between 4 and 5 miles long and the 12 Corp train under took to cut our train off but they did not do it. Captain let them pass there ammunition train and battery and they were bound to take there supply train through too, but our Captain told them that they could not go through until ours got passed and they swore that they would and drew out their swords. Captain ordered us to fix bayonets which we did in a short time and marched up to them and he told them to stop or he would charge bayonets on them; so they being afraid of us Jersey boys they stopped quick I tell you and we passed our train on. Captain Thompson is as brave man as we have got in our regiment and he showed no cowardice in the affair but stood his ground and we with him waiting for his command to charge on them. I expected that we should have a fight with them sure but they gave way and submitted to Captain Thompson; he is from Bridgeton I believe, and he is a lawyer when he is at home, but it don't matter what occupation he follows he is a fine man and looks to the well fare of his men. He has been acting as Major in our regiment since we have been on the march.

Tell Mrs. Strang that Dan Gaskill came back to the regiment and he looks as fat as ever I saw him look in my life and he marched with us five days and he was taken sick again on the road and the doctor sent him back to the hospital again and he has taken to spitting blood and I think that he will get his discharge from the regiment in a short time and be sent home.

As soon as we get encamped for the winter I am to have a furlough granted me for to come home and I hope that I may live to get it and then I can tell you all about it and the war. I have made another ring for Eliza and I will keep it until I come home as she had such bad luck not to get the other one that I sent her. No more at present but remain

Your Husband and Son
C. W. Gamble.

Write soon and often and tell me all about the draft in Pittstown.

Camp Near Bristolville, Virginia.
August 20th, 1863.

To my dear Wife Eliza;-

I now take my pen in hand to inform you that I am well at present and hope these few lines may find you and all the rest enjoying the same blessing. We have moved from the camp where I last wrote home and are now on the opposite side of Bristolville, from where we were encamped about 6 miles from our last camp ground and we have not got as nice a place as we had in the old camp. We had a splendid shade and a good stream of water for to wash our clothes in and we could bathe in the stream if we had a mind. It is healthy for us and now where we are we are exposed to the sun and in a very low place and no stream of water anywhere near us and we have very poor water to drink and I am in hopes that we will not have to stay here long.

This morning our boys are all gone out on picket; and I am left in the camp alone as I am corporal and commissary and am excused by the captain from all duties except the duties of commissary and that takes me about one hour every day which makes it very easy for me now. The morning we left our old camp I had a lame back and I thought that it was going to remain so for some time as I could hardly get up when I was down but I have recovered and I feel as well as ever.

Eliza I often think of you and my parents and friends and you always seem the nearest to my heart as I often dream of you when I am asleep, and when I wake in the morning my first thought is of you and home and I still feel in hopes that I may live through this war and get home, safe to you and my friends again. I received a letter from Annie this week and she said that they were all well. Dave got a letter from his son Charlie Smith last night and he stated in his letter that Isiah Dare had shot Uriah Wallen, and that Daddy

86

Van Gilder had been abused by some ruffians last week and it being the week of the camp I think these people in that neighborhood ought to think more of them selves at that time than to take the life of their fellow men and especially to fall upon as old a man as Mr. Van Gilder and I think that the place for such villains as them is in this war and in front of all the battles and to be kept under the strictest rules of the war and when not on duty kept in some close confinement at hard labor; for such I think I could have no mercy.

Eliza I would have liked to have been at home to have gone with you to camp but I am here in a far distant land from you endeavoring to protect a country that our fore fathers fought for and I have not the privilege of enjoying a camp-meeting with you but I hope that we both may live to enjoy one together again and I hope you did enjoy your self as well as you could with out my presence. Eliza write and let me know how you are getting along and how you enjoyed yourself during the camp.

I do not expect that we shall stay here but a few days; they say that we are going to Alexander but how true it is I can not tell but where ever we go I will write and let you know where I am. I have got some money but don't feel safe to send it by letter to you as I have no other way now but if you want any and let me know and I will risk it. I can not tell when they will commence granting furloughs but when they do I will get the first one and then I will come home and I think that Dave will come too. He is acting corporal in my place now. No more at present, but remain your loving Husband

C. W. Gamble.

Write to me as soon as you get this letter.

87

Camp on Elk Run, Virginia.
September 5th, 1863.

To My Dear Wife Eliza;-

I now sit down to take my pencil in hand to inform you that I received your letter on the 4th of this month and was pleased to hear from you; and to hear that you were all well and that you all were enjoying such good health. Your letter found me in good health but I was some what tired, as I had just come off a reconnoitering party and we had stayed three days and had marched 15 miles to get back to camp. I am always delighted to get a letter from you for it does me good to read them. I had been looking for a letter from you for some time and almost made up my mind that you had not got the letter that I wrote you, and our mail being robbed about that time I thought that your letter had been destroyed with the rest of them.

I was going to send you some money in that letter but I was afraid to risk it; as so many of our boys had sent money to their folks and they have not got it, and having no other way to send it at that time I thought that I would wait. Since then I have had a chance to send some the same way that I did before and I sent $50.00 again to Father. You stated in your letter that Father had not given you any of the money that I sent him; it is strange to me that he did not let you have some of it for I wrote to him to let you have $10 of it: for I don't think that you would spend it to any extravagance as some of the boys wives do.

I could have sent you more money than what I did, but I like to have some money by me to get some things to eat, so that I can have a change some times. Although we have to pay a big price for them, when my appetite calls for such things I think I might as well get some of them as we don't know what moment we may have to leave this unfriendly world, and I think that we ought to enjoy the luxuries of a soldiers life as far as possible without letting you and my creditors suffer by the transaction.

We have had all of our years pay but 2 months (it being one year yesterday since we were mustered in to the Service). My clothes and shoes this last year, including my first suit, amounts to $72.03 with what I have lost on the Campaign; and we are only allowed $42.00 worth in a year so you see I shall not have much coming to me the next three months if I should live to see the time out. Very nearly all of the boys that have been with us on this campaign have over run their bill and a great deal more than I have. But we mat have some deduction made for the clothes that we have lost and if we do it will make it better for us.

I have made up my mind that the best way is not to have any clothes, but the one suit; and when you want to wash a shirt pull it off and go without one till it gets dry. That is the way that we have been doing for sometime back and sometimes we do not have the time to dry them and have to put them on wet. If we were home and had to do it we could not stand it long before we would be in our graves; but I think that a soldier can stand anything. If I should live my three years through all of the hardships of a soldier's life I shall think that I can stand anything.

The weather is warm here in the day time but is very cold at night; and we sleep very cold some times. We have not got any woolen blankets as yet so we have nothing to cover ourselves with but our gum blankets and they are not worth much to keep us warm. But we try to do the best that we can these cold nights; Dave often growls because I don't lay closer to him, and says if I don't lay closer he will freeze to death.

We are getting so thin that are bones are getting so sharp that we dare not touch each other. We have to lay on the ground and that is so dry and hard that the skin is very nearly worn off of our hips. I have noticed that when the boys are in bathing and their breeches are off that their hips are all black and blue where they lay on them and some of them the skin is actually worn off of them.

When we leave this camp I can not tell where we shall go to. We have a talk in camp that we are going to have a fall campaign yet, but I hope it may not be the case for I am getting tired of marching and I want to get in winter quarters before it gets to cold. It is very dry here and we have the greatest time to get any water to drink, and when we do get it is so muddy, just like water out of a mud hole. We have to go a mile to wash our shirts and then have to wash them in a mud hole which leaves them not much cleaner than they were before. When the boys want to wash their clothes they come to me and I have to take them to the commander of the camp and get a pass for them to go out; and have to go with them to see that they return back or I am accountable for them.

I shall have to stop writing now as I am one of the committee to examine the Clothing Bills to see if they correspond with one another. Well I don't know that I have much more to say. Tell Mrs. Strang that the last time that I heard from Dan he was at the hospital at Washington and was about but not so as to go on duty. I don't think they will ever send him back to the regiment again; I think that they will put him on some light duty.

Ask Isaac Johnson if he got that letter that I sent to him if he did tell him to read it to you. Tell Dave DuBois I wrote 2 letters to him and he has not answered and I shall not write until he writes to me, for I know that he can write for I have seen him write. Tell Mother that I would like to have that pickle that she wanted to send me but I cannot tell how I shall get it. Tell Ella that I expect that she will be such a large girl when I come home that she won't hardly speak to me. Tell Sally and Aunt Abby that I send my best respects to them and Eli to tell him to write to me. Give my respects to all and don't forget any. No more at present. Good-bye

Your Affectionate Husband
C. W. Gamble.

Write and let me know how you get your county money. Tell Lide that I got her letter and wrote back an answer to it. Tell me what there is going on around home for I will find out if you don't tell me. C.W.G.

Sutlers Tent

Culpepper, Virginia
September 14th, 1863.

Dear Parents and Wife;-

I take my pencil in hand to inform you that I received your kind and welcome letter stating that you had received my check for $30; I also received two papers from Isaac Johnson with a little note in them stating that you were all well. I received them on the 9th at the old camp on Elk River, and they found me in good health and good spirits and I hope that these few lines will find you all the same.

We are now on the march after the enemy; we started on the 12th and we marched to Warrenton Station that night where we were drenched with a good shower of rain; about 11 o'clock at night I was called on to draw grub and a dark night it was for me to attend to my duty and I being waked from a sound sleep I did not hardly get my eyes open until I got to the commissary department.

I had a rough road to travel in the morning it being Sunday. We started on our march and we soon began to hear the roar of cannon telling us that the fight had began. We marched on until we came to the next station called Brandy Station where we captured two horses and a keg of whiskey and a box of tobacco and two Rebs, supposed to be guerillas; one of them was a citizen of the place and had a wife and 4 small children; it looked hard to take their Father away from them as his wife and children begged for him, but we had to take him with us; two of his children followed him for a mile and then they were forced to go back. We marched on soon seeing the affects of a battle fought by our calvary and artillery; seeing pieces of shells and dead horses and some dead Rebs and large trees cut off by the shells telling us that we were close to the enemy.

We arrived at this place about six o'clock where we were drawn up in line of battle right in front of the town of Culpepper which our

92

forces took to day and captured four pieces of artillery and about 100 of the Rebs. After we formed the line of battle we stacked arms and Dave and myself pitched our tent and got our suppers and laid down for the night, where I rested comfortably for the night. Dave did not rest very well as he has been unwell for some time and has to get up several times during the night.

This morning we got up and went to the run and got some water and I got breakfast, and all being quiet yet I thought that I would write to you, but we do not know how soon we may be called on to go into battle; it may be before you receive this letter I may be laid under the soil of Virginia, and if it should be the case it will be fighting for my country; but I am in hopes that it may not be the case with me.

Sam Green has got back with us and is with us now; he got a letter from his mother yesterday and one from his uncle W. Bowers. Sam's wound is healed up and he looks hearty. It is very foggy here this morning. No more at present. Good-bye.

From Your Son and Husband
C. W. Gamble.

Write soon and as often as you can. (Direct as before)

To My Dear Wife;-

I now sit down in my tent to write you a few lines to inform you that I received your kind and welcome letter and also one from Mary Watson; and was glad to hear that you were all well and your letters found me in good health and spirits. I am now alone in my tent; Dave was taken sick on the march and fell out and I have not seen him nor heard tell of him since, but I suppose that he is in some hospital before this time. I feel very lonesome with out him as we were always together since we have been in the army. He looked very bad and was very weak when he left us. Tell Lib I got the letter that she sent to him and when I find out where he is I will send it to him for I think that he will write right away to me as soon as he gets to some hospital.

We are now encamped on a hill in front of the enemy and in sight of them. Our Cavalry are skirmishing with them every day; our regiment is in front as usual supporting the battery where there is the most danger of being hit with the shells. We have had to take the front in all of the battles that we have been in. It seems to me that our General dare not trust any one of the other regiments in front he says that we are the brave boys and he dare trust us any where; for he believes we are no cowards and says we have to take the front here in the battles and if we live to get home we must take the front there. We expect to go in a fight every day but the enemy seems to be afraid to attack us and they keep falling back all the time and we are advancing on them all the time and they may be tolling us into their fortifications, and then they will attack us and give us battle.

Since we have been on the march our Cavalry has taken the town of Culpepper and the Orange and Alexander R.R. and the cars are running now. We marched through the town of Culpepper with our flags flying and the citizens gave us many a black look.

Yesterday we (the whole brigade) were marched out to see 2 deserters shot. They were substitutes belonging to the 14th Connecticut Regiment in our corps; and it was an awful sight to see. The Corp was formed in a square with one end open and the two men were marched in to the center of the square with their 2 coffins a head of them carried by 4 men and the men that were to shoot them were behind the coffins; each man was locked arms with a minister and one of them had his Father on the other side of him. When they came to the place of execution they were placed on their coffins with their hands tied behind them and a handkerchief tied over their eyes; then the men that had to shoot them were marched within ten paces of them and not a word was said to them (the command was given to them by a wave of the captain's sword) and they fired but did not kill them dead. They then marched up to them and shot again, and then they did not kill one of them and his Father told them to give him another load when the captain stepped up and drew his revolver and killed him. After he was dead his Father took charge of him and took him home with him; they both belong to Connecticut I believe. I tell you it was a sad sight and a warning to all deserters in our army.

We have had plenty of rain since we have been on the march; it has rained every day and we have had several drenching; it makes it bad for us at night the ground being so wet and muddy and our loads getting wet it makes them heavy for us to carry. I being commissary yet I do not have very heavy duties to do only when I have to draw grub after night and it being dark nights it makes it bad for me.

You stated in your letter that you would send me a shirt if I wanted one; it will be very acceptable to me if you want to send me one. Some of the boys have had some splendid shirts sent to them; the women joined together and made them; they are flannel and woolen and are braided and buttons on in the style with a pocket on each side. If they will send me one I will be very thankful to you and them for it.

We live on raw pork and hard tack on the march and when we encamp where a corn field is we have plenty of corn. I think that when we are encamped our boys will average about 10 bushels or ears in a day and it don't take them long to destroy a field of corn. I dare not eat much of it as it does not agree with me. I have not seen a watermelon nor a citron nor a ripe peach this season and a very few apples and not seeing them I do not have any appetite for them. They are now planting a battery right in front of my tent and I think that they are going to send a few shells over towards the enemy to see if they can tell where they are and if we can not find them I think that we shall cross the Rapidan after them some time to day.

Tell Mary Watson that I will write an answer to her letter in a few days if I don't get killed. I don't know as I have any more to tell you this time so I will bring my letter to a close by saying Good-bye to you all. Give my love to all inquiring friends.

I would like for you to send me some more stamps if it is convenient for you to do so. Let Father read this letter for it will answer for both this time as we are on the march and have not much chance to write. Send me a map of Virginia if you can get one with out much trouble. C.W. Gamble.

From Your Affectionate Husband till death
C. W. Gamble

Hanging a Deserter
(William Johnson)

Photo courtesy the Library of Congress

Dear Parents and Wife;-

I take my pencil in hand to inform you that I am well at present and hope that these few lines may find you all enjoying the same good blessing. I have been looking for a letter from you for all the week and have not received any from you. I received one from Dave Smith's wife (for him) last week and one this week and I have got them both yet, because I do not know where to send them as I do not know where he is. I have not seen nor heard tell of him since he left me at Cedar Mountain 10 days ago. I expected that he would have written to me before this time to let me know where he is but I have not had any word from him yet. I carry my whole tent with me and put up by my self.

We now have to carry eight days rations with us and my tent and woolen blanket and gum blanket two haversacks frying pan, hatchet, knapsack, tin cup 60 rounds of cartridges and canteen altogether makes me a load to march with; but we don't march more than from 2 to 6 miles a day. We can see the enemy all the time but have not made any attack on them as yet and what we are waiting for I cannot tell.

Very nearly all of the regiment are out on duty now and we haven't but 2 men left in camp besides us uncommissioned officers and there are but three of us and our Lieutenant. Last night we were called out in line in front of our camp at eight o'clock and had to lay on our arms until morning; expecting the enemy to open on us as they had been stirring around quite briskly yesterday, but they did not open on us.

There is a nice farm in front of us between the lines and the General says that there is peaches on the farm, plenty of them, and he knows that the boys would like to have some of them; and he says that he is going to take us over there. If he starts over there with us our boys will do some sharp fighting as we are very fond of peaches and we have not had any this summer. I got a taste last night; there was two of our boys got a box sent to them and it had some peaches in it and they gave me one, the only ripe peach I have had this summer. We have had plenty of roast and boiled corn until now it has got too hard for us to roast or boil so they have began to feed it to the horses. I am in my old business of commissary and will not have to draw any grub for 8 days; that leaves me no duty to do unless we get into a fight and then I have to go in with the rest of the boys.

I wrote a letter to Eliza, my wife, since I wrote to you and she has not written to me since. I would like to receive a letter from you or her once a week any way and not to fail in doing so and I will write back again to you. I would like for you to see Mr. McIntosh and ask him if he could make me a pair of boots with high legs for this winter as I will have to have a pair and there is no chance to have them made here. If he can tell him to make them out of stout calf skin and I will send him the money for them. I got me a pair made last winter at Ellicott's Mills; if he can make them you can send them to me in a box as some of our boys are getting them now.

I would like to know whether you got those papers that I sent you. Tell Eliza if she sends them shirts by mail to let the ends of the shirts stick out and it will not cost as much, for they can see what they are, if the ends show. Tell Aunt Liddie that I got her letter and will write to you soon. Tell her that Sam is here and is as fat as a hog and says that he can not get enough to eat and he is the same old Sam yet and makes some very dry speeches for the boys to laugh at; and they all make a great account of Sam and think a great deal of him; when he came back to the regiment he came in the night and some of the boys had gone to bed and them that were up hollered "Sam Green has got back" and the boys all got up to see him. I think that he had a grin on his face for 15 minutes and they were as well pleased as if he had been there brother. He says that his arm is very tender yet where the ball went through it. He says that he would have liked to have got home on a furlough while he was in the hospital but he could not get one. He says that Enos Garrison took a French one or he would not have got home; and he says before he takes a French furlough he will stay his time out and I am sure that I should do the same.

I think if I should live I will get home on a furlough this Fall or Winter and I shall try hard for it as I would like to see you all again. Time seems to slip away very fast here too, but it seems to me as if it has been a long time since I left home. I do not know as I have much more to say this time, but there is one thing that I will say and that is that I want to get out of the state of Va. As I am getting tired of traveling in it and shant want to see it again if I get out of it. There is some nice timber in it and plenty of game and we have seen plenty of it but we dare not shoot any as we are not allowed to fire off our guns unless we are in battle. I must now close by saying Good-bye

Your Son and Husband
C. W. Gamble.

Union Artillery crossing The Rapidan River.

Camp near Culpepper, Virginia.
October 1ˢᵗ, 1863.

Dear Brother and Sister;-

I take my pen in hand to pen you a few lines to let you know that I am well and in good spirits yet and I hope that these few lines will find you and your little family in the same state of health. Conover got a letter from your place the other day and he said that you sent your respects to me stating that you were both well and that your baby grew like a pig and I do expect that you begin to feel quite motherly by this time. I would like to see you with your little one in your lap and see if you look motherly and if I should live to get home I will come down and see you.

Bob when I do come I want to make a trip with you to the oyster beds as I have not had any since I have been in the army and I think that I can get a good supply of them as I think that it will take no small quantity to supply me as I am very fond of them.

I got a letter from home last night and it stated that they were all well and that Eliza my wife was going to send me a shirt in the next mail and if you wish to send me anything by mail send me a neck handkerchief or a necktie or something like that and I can get it.

I wrote a letter to Rachel yesterday and shall write one to Annie this week. I have not heard from her since she was at Father's. Give my best respects to Mr. And Mrs. Mayhew and tell them that I am well yet and enjoying a soldiers life as well as he could expect considering the hardships that we have to pass through. Tell them that I have been in two hard battles and got hit both times but not seriously we have one of the hardest campaigns this summer that is on record; we have marched 800 miles since we started on the march. We started on the first of June and we are not in winter quarters yet and I can not tell when we shall get in them; but I hope that we will soon get to them as it is getting quite cold here at

100

nights. We have encamped on a hill in a large piece of woods in front of the enemy and can see them doing picket duty.

My duties are very light for me as I am corporal and commissary of the Company and excused from all duties except the duties as a commissary. We have plenty of squirrels here and I have seen as high as six on one tree and have seen two flocks of white wild turkeys but I saw them and that was all for they were out of my sight as quick as a flash. We are not allowed to shoot them or I would have had some squirrel soup and a turkey dinner before this time.

We have had it quite quiet in our lines till night before last when we went out to put out our pickets we thought that we would extend them out a little further and the Rebs thought that they would not let us do that; so we were ordered out in line and marched about a mile from camp and halted our cavalry then made a charge on them and they skedaddled like them wild turkeys did. We then marched out to the lines on double quick and laid down on our stomachs and waited an hour expecting them to advance on us but they did not come. We then extended our picket line out and the remainder of us were marched into camp where we rested quiet for the night.

We have it dry and warm in the day time and cold at nights but we have plenty of good rails to build fires with; and we do not spare them. We have had plenty of corn to boil till now it has got to hard for us, but we have got a way of grinding it. We make our own mills and they are composed of a piece of tin punched full of holes, that forms a grater we run the ears up and down the grater and that makes the meal and we make some good cakes out of it and it is finer than any miller can grind it. As my paper is getting scarce and I will have to close by saying good-bye

From your brother
C. W. Gamble.

Write soon.

101

Camp near Culpepper, Virginia
October 2nd, 1863.

Dear Brother and Sister;-

I take my pen in hand to inform you that I am well and enjoying as good health as can be expected as a soldier's life and I hope that these few lines may find you and your family enjoying the same good health. We are considered on the march yet and haven't ended our summer campaign but I hope that we will soon get into Winter Quarters where we can make ourselves comfortable for the Winter. We have traveled over 800 miles since the 1st of June.

We are now encamped on a hill in front of the Rebels and can see them; we are doing picket duty. We are in a piece of large timber and the squirrels are very thick here; I have seen as high as 6 on one tree and I have seen 2 flocks of wild turkeys since I have been here. I saw them and that was all for they were out of my sight as quick as a flash we are not allowed to shoot or I would have had some squirrel soup and a turkey dinner before this time.

I wrote a letter to Rachel and one to Eliza this week and I thought that I must write to you too. I saw 2 deserters shot in our corps the other day and it was a sad sight to look at; they belonged to the 14th Connecticut and was from the town of Connecticut; one of them had his Father with him and he took it very hard. I for one part don't want to see any more shot.

My duty is very easy yet as I am commissary of the Company and am excused from all other duty. We have had it very quiet here until last Tuesday night when we went to put our pickets out and wanted to extend our lines and the Rebs thought that they would not let us do it so we were ordered out in line of battle and marched down to the lines and our cavalry made a charge on them and they skedaddled as fast as them turkeys that I saw. We loaded and laid down and waited about an hour expecting that they would advance on us but they did not come so we extended our pickets and the remainder of us returned to camp where we rested for the night and it has been very quiet ever since.

We have it dry here and warm in the day time and cold at night but we have plenty of fence rails and we don't spare them on our fires. This morning it is raining and looks as if we will have 2 or 3 days storm and that makes it bad for us as it is so muddy in a wet time. We have had plenty of corn to boil since we have been here but now it is getting to hard so we have got a way of grinding it and make cakes of it and we make our own mills and the way we make our mills we take a piece of tin and punch holes in it and nail it on a piece of board and run the ears of corn up and down and this grates it and that makes the meal and it is finer than any that I ever saw ground at a grist mill; I grind my corn and bake cakes enough for breakfast in 15 minutes and some of the boys have made pumpkin pies too as we have plenty of them around here.

I got a letter from home yesterday and they were all well and Eliza said that she was going to send me a nice shirt by mail and I shall be glad to get it as the shirts that we get in the army are so rough for me to wear that they keep me scratching all of the time and I do believe that they breed lice where a flannel shirt will not and 1 skirmish every day as we call it here to keep them off of me as they are very numerous in the army.

We do expect to go in battle every day as they, the Rebs, intend to attack us and if they do we will whip them if we can. My paper is getting scarce so I will have to quit writing by bidding you all good-bye. Give my love to the children and kiss them all for me.

> From Your Loving Brother
> C. W. Gamble.

Camp near Culpepper, Virginia.
October 5th, 1863

Dear Eliza;-

I take my pen in hand to inform you that I am well at present and hope these few lines will find you and all the rest in the same state of health, and also to inform you that I received the shirt and a note from Elizabeth Smith stating that Dave was at the Washington Hospital; and she wished me to send his letters to him. I received a few lines from E. A. Rand, Delegate of the Christian Commission, stating that he requested me to send them to him so I sealed them in another envelope and sent them to the place that he directed me too ; he was at that time at Culpepper 2nd Corps Hospital. I have not heard whether he got them or not, but I would like to hear from him for I would like to know how he is coming along by this time; I would like him to get well and return to his regiment, for I am very lonesome with out him as we always tented together ever since we have been in the army, and always got along like brothers. I hope he may be able to return soon, but while he is at the Hospital I hope he may get a furlough to come home, for I think it might do him good to see his family, and probably settle his mind. I think that he thought a great deal of home which was part of his trouble.

The shirt you sent me I got last night and was happy to receive it, as I expect it was made by your own hands and I don't think it will rip to pieces like some that they get to the Sutlers; several of the boys have bought shirts of him and they rip to pieces right away, and they pay a big price for them. Such a shirt as you sent me he charges $6.00 for, and I could have got $6.00 for mine as quick as I unwrapped it. They offered that to me for it. I tried the shirt on this morning and it fits first rate, but the pocket is to low down by the length of them, and there is no buttons on them. I would like to have buttons on them so I can button them so as to keep my things

104

from falling out of my pockets when I am laying down; but I can sew them on as I see you sent me a needle.

We have had orders this morning to move and I shall soon be busy drawing rations, as it is a hard job to draw rations and I deal them out when we are going to move. We have to draw three days more rations and we have eight days rations on hand now, and three days more will make eleven days rations that we will have to start with which will make our loads heavy for us to carry. Where we are going to I can not tell, but I think we are going to leave the front and move back towards Culpepper and let some other Corps take our place.

Well orders have come to draw grub so I shall have to attend to it, so you will have to excuse me for this time. We received our pay again last Saturday and after taking out my clothes bill I only had $3.94 coming to me, so I can not send you any money this time but I will next time. So I will close by saying good-bye

From Your Husband,
C. W. Gamble.

P.S. Write soon. Sam Green has been sick but has got better again. He received $70.00 this pay day. Give my love to all inquiring friends and tell them I want to hear from them soon.

On the Bull Run Battlefield
October 17th, 1863.

Dear Parents and Wife;-

I now take my pen in hand to inform you that I am still a live, but not enjoying very good health at this present time; having been on the march for ten days, traveling day and night, and it has been raining a good part of the time, I have caught a very heavy cold, and having the rheumatism in my back, makes me feel very bad and one time I thought I would have to fall out, but my ambition was great enough to let me continue on the march.

We have had two battles with the enemy during the march and drove them both times. We had one in the morning commencing about 6 o'clock and lasted till about 10 o'clock; we then started for a place that is well fortified, but before we reached that place we came across the enemy again in front of us on the same day about half past three o'clock; we were ordered to make a charge on them, and we did it on the double quick, and the Rebs seeing us coming after them they could not stand it, so they flanked to the right and formed a line of battle and we flanked to the left and formed our line. The 14th Connecticut were in front; they opened fire on them and the Rebs began to fall all along the line, and we had a sharp time for about fifteen minutes; then they fell back; we then made another charge on them and captured three pieces of artillery and several prisoners. Our battery then opened on them and we soon drove them again. It then being night both parties stopped firing and laid down to rest.

We had not laid down more than thirty minutes, before we were ordered up to march on. We got up and started on the doublequick for a mile, fording a stream about three feet deep, and marched about 8 miles to the place where we are now. We got here about 3 o'clock in the morning, and rested till about 6 o'clock when we made our coffee, having nothing else to eat, and nothing the day before. I had 7 crackers and I made them last me three days, I having had my haversack knapsack and gun stole the other day before the battle; I went to the Major and got permission to hunt for them, and succeeded in finding my knapsack, but did not get my haversack or gun. On the morning of the battle the Major brought me another gun, (they were stolen when I was after water).

Yesterday our wagons got to us and I drew grub again and we now have plenty; the boys seem quite cheered up again. Day before yesterday the Rebs opened on us again, and our batteries commenced firing on them which soon stopped their fire, and drove them again. Yesterday we had a large force of the regular cavalry from Washington come in here and they made a raid out about 4 miles, but did not find any Rebs. This morning the sun rose clear and the wind is more west which makes it a fine morning; our army lies in a fine position for battle at any time, and I do not think we can be drove from it.

We are planting some large guns at Centerville, which is about 3 miles distant. I think that we will make a stand here for a while. We had a very hard march to get here, as both armies were making for this position, and, lucky for us, we got here before the Rebs, and they say we can (that is the 2 corps) lick Lees whole army now on this ground we occupy. It is called old Bull Run Battle ground.

My back has got better, but I have got a heavy cold; my eyes run with water, and with the rest I have had a large boil on my hip, and that has been a bother to me too, but it has broke now and it feels better. I hope these few lines may find you all in good health. We had some killed and several wounded in the three battles, but I have escaped yet. I here some firing on the right but what it will amount to, I can not tell yet. No more at present. Good-bye; write soon.

> From your Son and Husband
> C. W. Gamble.

GENERAL GOUVERNEUR K. WARREN.
PHOTOGRAPHED BY MATHEW BRADY

Camp on the Warrenton Branch R.R.
In sight of the Town of Warren, Va.
October 24th, 1863.

Dear Parents and Wife;-

I take my pencil in hand to write to you to inform you that I received a letter from you on the 16th, dated the 11th, and it found me in good health, considering the hard march and the three fights we had to go through, and the heavy loads that we had to carry; I hope these few lines may find you all in good health.

We do now expect to make our winter quarters here, if nothing turns up more than we know of at present. It is a very nice place and we can get plenty of wood and are close by the Rail-Road where we can get our supplies handily.

We have been in three battles since we have been on the march, and one very sharp one, but we drove them every time. The hardest fight was close to Warrenton Junction; the rebs got ahead of us expecting to cut us off, but we proved to be too much for them for we cut our way through them. The 14th Connecticut being ahead of us they were in the battle first; they fired two volleys at them and were then ordered to make a charge, which they did, and the Rebs turned tail too and run. We had some killed and several wounded, but the dead Rebels laid very thick on the field. We were in the line of battle on the left wing, and they did not come out on us, but went around in the rear of us; and it being now night we were marched behind the batteries and laid down on our arms.

We laid there about two hours, when General Warren found out that the Rebs were trying to get ahead of us again, and making for Bull Run to cut us off there; so we were ordered up and marched on to get to the Battle ground at Bull Run before them, which we succeeded in doing. We got there about daylight and a nice position it was too. About ten o'clock the Rebs opened their battery on us;

our battery soon opened on them, which silenced there batteries very quick. We laid under the fire of both batteries all the time some of the Reb's shells bursted close by us, but did not hit any of us; we soon drove them again and followed on after them, and encamped on the same ground they did the night before. In the morning we heard that the main part of the army had crossed the Rappahannock again, so we made ourselves contented again for the day. Our boys enjoyed themselves by going on the battle ground and picking up guns and equipments as it was close by.

I escaped again without a scratch. Sam Green was hit with a ball again in the temple and knocked down flat, and never broke the line; we were going up to the Rebs on the double quick at the time, and I being in front did not see him fall; when we stopped they told me Sam was killed. I looked around to see where he was, and I saw him coming; I went to him and found he was not hurt badly but the ball had raised a large lump. I think the ball hit his cap brim, and that was the reason the skin was not broken. Sam and myself both saw George and he is well and all right yet and he said he could not get any one to write or he would have wrote before.

It is raining hard now and I will have to stop by saying Good-bye to you all,

> From your son and husband
> C. W. Gamble.

P.S. Write to me soon and don't forget. I have been troubled about Dave Smith very much since his death, for he was so much like a brother to me, and I think he suffered a great deal.

Dear Parents and Wife;-

I now sit down to endeavor to write a few lines to inform you that I have received two letters from you; one from Father and from you and they both found me not in good health. I have had a hard turn of the diarrhea for four weeks and have been under the doctors hands for three weeks but have not been in the hospital yet. The doctor wanted me to go to the hospital but I would not give up to go for I don't want to go there if I can help it.

When we are on the march I get my pass from the doctor and take my own time for it, and when I get tired I can sit down and rest. The doctor would not allow me to eat meat of any kind or drink coffee for two weeks; so I bought some tea and sugar and cheese when I can get it and butter, but they are all very scarce and hard to get down here and I have to pay a price for them.

I think I fell away 20 lbs. in two weeks; the captain says if I keep on falling away there will be nothing of me in a little while but the doctor allows me to eat meat but not much so I think maybe I can recruit up again in a little while; I don't feel quite as well this morning as I felt yesterday but I thought I must try to write to you and let you know how I was getting along.

How long we shall stay in this place I can not tell. This place is called Milton and we are on the Fritz Lee property, the son of General Lee, the one that they was going to hang some time ago. They say we are waiting for them to get the Rail-Road fixed up and that will take about two weeks and then we will go into winter quarters and when we do get in quarters I want you to send me another box of things. You stated in your letter Dave had taken some buckwheat to the mill to get ground; tell him to send me some of the flour in the box when you send it, and some yeast and I can bake them myself. I would like for you to send me some more black thread as I have to mend my clothes so much they being made with those sewing machines they rip all to pieces and I can not get more thread here; it is begging a great deal but I can not help it but I will make it all right if I live to get home again.

Eliza, you stated you wanted to see me, I dare say you do but not worse than I want to see you and all the rest of you. But I am not allowed that privilege. We have some very cold weather here and have nothing but our little tents to put up in, and can not have any fire in them; it makes it very cold to sleep of nights.

Broadwater puts up with me now and we do the best we can do to keep warm. This will have to answer both letters this time; and I will write more the next as I am not well yet so Good-bye

From your son and husband
Charles W. Gamble.

My head is affected so I can hardly write, so you will have to excuse me this time so Good-bye.

William Henry Fitzhugh Lee
1837-1891
Son of Robert E. Lee

Milton, Virginia, out on picket
November 20th, 1863.

Dear Parents and Wife;-

I take my pencil in hand to inform you that I received your kind and welcome letter this morning and the package of thread, paper and needles; and a very welcome message it was to me. It found me on my post on duty with 12 men in my charge on picket, as we have to put out strong pickets out here. My health is as good as can be expected considering the sickness that I have been laboring under for some time; I have a good appetite, and feel very well with the exception of my limbs and joints; they are stiff and swelled some yet which I think is caused by the medicine that I have been taking.

This is the first time that I have been on duty for some time and would not have been on this time, but I offered to go, for I thought it would help me some to go out as it was nice weather, and not far to march; and if I do not get more cold I think I will be all right in a few days, if I can get the medicine out of my joints.

I bought a few parsnips and potatoes and made a stew yesterday and I tell you it seemed like home to get them and I had a good dinner, I tell you. A few days ago I bought a small head of cabbage and made some soup and that was good too, but it was only by chance that I got them.

You wished to know in the letter if I got the map; I got it the same week you sent it and thought that I had written to you that I had received it before this time. Everything that you have sent me I believe that I have received yet. As quick as we get in Winter Quarters I want you to send me the box; you said that you wanted to mention the articles; I have no particular articles; send me anything that will not spoil the box within a week, for I think that it will take it that long to get to me. If you send me any pickles or pepper send them in tin cans or jars and they wont sour the rest of the things in the box. If you send me pies wrap them up in paper. Well dried beef or ham will keep any how. Tell Martha, Dave DuBois' wife to send me some pickled cherries if she has got them. Send me anything but pork and hard tack, for we have got them. I think you might venture to start the box within a week, for I shall be sure to get it if I am alive, for it will come to the regiment for we will be along the railroad all the time. Don't forget the buckwheat flour; send me two or three quarts.

Through my faithfulness as a soldier I am about to be promoted to the rank of Sergeant of the Company and show you and all of my friends that I am a true and faithful soldier to my country and office (self praise, as the saying says, is no praise at all) but I must tell you what I am as there is so many uncommissioned officers that do not do their duty as officers; for my own part I have always tried to do my duty and to please my officers the best that I know how, and to salute them correctly and show them that I am a soldier and not playing soldier in time of war and under their commands; and so doing I may be able to gain their good will.

While I was sick in my tent William Brown was sick in the tent with me both handled in the same way; he went to the hospital and was taken worse and died. I did not go and now I am spared and getting well as fast as can be expected. He died at the head quarter hospital I believe; whether he has been sent or taken home I can not tell, but I suppose that you know by this time. As my paper is scarce I will have to close, so good-bye to you all; hoping this letter may find you all well; write soon,

From Your Affectionate Son
C. W. Gamble.

I feel very lonesome some time with no Dave to talk too.

Stevensburg, Virginia.
December 12th, 1863.

Dear Parents and Wife;-

I now take my pencil in hand to write you a few lines to ask you to excuse me for not writing to you before this time. We have been on the march for some time and have stopped to put up Winter Quarters, and have stockaded three times before this and have had to leave them. I have been so unwell and so busy when I felt like writing that I have not had the time to write; but now I thought that I must write a few lines to let you know how I was getting along. I am not well now but am as well as can be expected considering the bad weather here and the kind of fare we have to put up with. We have it wet and cold and have to carry wood for a half of mile.

Broadwater and myself have both been sick for some time and we have not got into stockade yet but I think we will be able to do it in a few days and then we will live more comfortably.

I hope that these few lines may find you all in good health. Well, Father I received my box that you sent me to day and everything arrived safely and I had not ate anything for three days and it came acceptable to me. There was nothing in the box but what tasted good to me and I hope that I may soon get home to reward you and my friends for it. The box had been opened but nothing had been touched in it. The mince pies were delicious. Broey and myself ate one quick and by the time that we had a taste of everything in the box we had a good dinner. To night we are going to have some buckwheat cakes and sausage for supper. Tell all of my friends that had a hand in the box that I am much obliged to them for their kindness to me and hope that I may get home to reward them for it. Tell Mr. Pedrick I am very much obliged to him for those nice apples he sent me and they were the nicest I have seen since I have been in the army. Tell him that I am going to write to him as soon as I can get myself fixed comfortable quarters and tell him all about the war and what I have experienced in it since I have been out.

I have a good bit to write to you about our fall campaign but don't feel like writing it now so you will have to excuse me for this time. If I should live you may see me this winter but you need not look for me until you see me and when you do you may not know me for I am nothing hardly but skin and bones at this present time. Well I must stop writing. Good bye to you all,

From Your Son and Husband,
C. W. Gamble.

WRITE SOON.

Camp Cooking
Photo courtesy of the Library of Congress

Hospital 12th N.J.V.
Near Stevensburg, Va.
December 21st, 1863.

My Dear Wife and Parents;-

I received your welcome letter of the 17th last night and now take pleasure in writing to you once more. As you will see from the heading of this letter that it is written from the Hospital. I was entered this morning. I had been sick for some time, and finding that I was not getting any better the Doctor put me in the Hospital where I can have better care taken of me than I would have while with the Company.

I have had the Diarrhea for some time so that I was getting very weak and thin and I began to think that I should never see you any more. I felt as though my grave would be dug in this state Virginia over which we have passed so much. But now I hope that I may soon be better and able to do my duty as in the past. The Doctor told me yesterday that I had what seemed to be Palpitation of the heart beside my other complaint, but he has not said anything about it since and I hope that it may pass away.

About your inquiry about money you need not send any as I have sufficient for all my wants. So that I can buy any little thing outside I may need while sick.

Hearing that Sam Green was reported killed in the fight at Bristow Station I will here take the opportunity of denying it as he is in the Company now being well and hearty and doing his duty regularly. He was hit in the temple in that fight and stunned for a short time but he has not suffered any from it.

Tell sister that she need not send me a box till I send her word again. Hoping to hear from you soon, I remain as ever

Yours affectionately
Charles W. Gamble.

117

Hospital N.J.V.
Near Stevensburg, Virginia
January 13th, 1864.

Mrs. Gamble.
Dear Madam;-

I embrace this opportunity of addressing a few lines to you to inform you of the sorrowful news that your husband has deceased. He departed this life this morning at twenty minutes to nine o'clock; he died a happy death with a smile on his face and I think by this time his spirit is in a better land where there is no more wars or sorrow, but peace and happiness forever.

I expect that it will be a sudden stroke to you but you may weep tears of joy to think he will meet you in Heaven. I was conversing with him last night and he requested me to give his things to John Broadwater. I wish when you answer this letter to state in it whether I shall give them to him or wait until some one should come on. His request was that he should be buried in a box and his body sent home if it could be done. The Doctors and us did all we could do for him and he was satisfied that we had.

Yours truly,
Thomas L. King.

N.B. When you answer this direct your letter to me 12th Regiment N.J.Vol. in care of the Hospital Steward. I would like for you to answer this as soon as it is convenient for you to do so.

Yours truly,
Thomas L. King.

Authors Note: The Military records said Charles died of Typhoid Fever near Stony Mountain, Virginia January 13, 1864.

Author's conclusion:

The Civil War of 1861-1865 was the most horrific and deadly for American citizens of all the wars the United States has been involved in. Six hundred twenty thousand soldiers and an unknown number of civilians were tragically killed. One quarter of the country's male population was destroyed.

I greatly admire and respect the courage and convictions of all these soldiers. Both the North and the South felt they were fighting for a just cause. The soldiers of both the Union and the Confederate side deserve to be remembered and honored for their patriotism.

But was this horrible war really necessary? Perhaps this costly tragic war could have been averted if President Abraham Lincoln and Congress would have rectified the legitimate grievances of the South. They should have made the system of taxes and disbursements fairer for the southern states. And Lincoln should have honored "States Rights" as provided for in the Constitution. I do understand Lincoln's noble and tremendous desire to keep the Union intact, but his flagrant violations of the Constitution led to so much unnecessary misery and death.

History books leave many people with the impression that the South rebelled mainly so they could keep the inhumane institution of slavery intact; that the North had to "preserve the Union" and that President Lincoln demanded the freeing of all the slaves. But the actual facts have been suppressed and the "official propaganda" has now been presented to the people for 150 years.

A more accurate term for the Civil War would be "The War for Southern Independence." The southern states had no desire to conquer the Union but rather only wanted to peaceably secede. Eleven southern states simply and peacefully disengaged from the union in which they had originally freely joined. Up until the time of the Civil War, it was generally understood by the citizens, government officials and the press that the states had a right to secede if the federal government no longer represented their best interests. This was considered another "Check and Balance" our founding fathers incorporated into the Constitution to keep an out of control federal government from stripping the states of their sovereign rights. In fact there were some legislators who feared that states would secede and unsuccessfully proposed a constitutional amendment to make it illegal. Since this amendment was never enacted, it is reasonable to assume that the states do have the right to secede. Remember, the states created the Federal Government as an agent or servant of the states. To voluntarily join the federation of states means these states had a right to withdraw from this union.

In fact, the Declaration of Independence states that governments derive their just powers from the consent of the governed, and in 1860 Southerners no longer consented to being governed by Washington DC. President Lincoln was against the South's decision to secede mainly because he did not want to lose revenue to the North from the South's decision to lower their tariffs on imports. He wanted to force the South back into the Union, but he didn't have the needed support of the northern citizens so he tricked the South into firing the first shot. Lincoln had promised to honor the armistice of not sending supplies and more soldiers to Fort Sumter which was in the newly declared Confederate States of America. But Lincoln secretly sent his ships there in the middle of the night. This provocation on southern soil caused the South to fire the first shot. The North then stated that the South was the instigator of an armed rebellion and the South stated that they were merely defending themselves against the invaders. To force the South back into the Union, Lincoln's armies ended up killing about 300,000 southern Americans--one out of every four males aged 20 to 40 years old.

The South's decision to secede can best be summed up with the term, "States Rights." This included slavery issues but even more important was the unfair monetary issues imposed upon the South by the Federal Government. Contrary to what most people believe, the preservation of the institution of slavery was *not* the primary cause for the South's desire for independence. In fact, The

120

Constitution of the Confederate States of America prohibited the importation of slaves. [Article 1, Section 9]

> **The Constitution of the Confederate States of America**
> *Section 9 - Limits on Congress, Bill of Rights*
> *1. The importation of Negroes of the African race from any foreign country other than the slaveholding States or Territories of the United States of America is hereby forbidden; and Congress is required to pass such laws as shall effectually prevent the same.*

Slavery would have surely ended before long without engaging in a Civil War--Numerous other countries in the 19th century were able to end slavery without a civil war. Confederate President Jefferson Davis even said in a speech that he thought slavery in America would disappear within two generations.

Yet many people today believe the war was fought because Abraham Lincoln wanted to "free the slaves." But the most common rallying call in the north was "Preserve the Union", not "Free the Slaves". In fact, Lincoln stated that if he could preserve the Union without freeing a single slave he would do that. His only concern was to keep the federation of states intact.

Many people believe Abraham Lincoln's Emancipation Proclamation of 1863 was a law which freed all the slaves. But the proclamation was actually only "a war measure" as Lincoln put it. (to punish the South) The war had been going on for over a year and a half at this point. Emancipation would take place only in rebel states not under Union control. The London Spectator recognized it as a brilliant propaganda tactic. In the edition of October 11, 1862 it was written, "The principle [of the proclamation] is not that a human being cannot justly own another, but that he cannot own him unless he is loyal to the United States." Lincoln's Emancipation Proclamation did not free a single slave. I have been unsuccessful to find any credible document listing the names, location and dates of any slaves that were set free at this time. I am not sure what the federal government would have done with them. They couldn't have been sent to Abraham Lincoln's home state of Illinois because there had been a law passed in Illinois not allowing any more

Negros to move into that state. The slaves were not actually freed, in both the North and South, until 1865 when the 13th Amendment was passed.

Yes, slavery was wrong, but that wasn't the reason Lincoln fought the Civil War. The real reason the business and political leaders in the north were so intent on keeping the southern states in the union was a monetary concern. If they allowed the South to secede, they would not have enough money to fund government expenditures because the source--tariffs on imports to the southern ports--would not be available. In addition, tariffs raised the price of imported goods to a level where the less efficient manufacturers in the northeast could be competitive. The former Vice President John C. Calhoun aptly stated, "The North had adopted a system of revenue and disbursements in which an undue proportion of the burden of taxation has been imposed upon the South, and an undue proportion of its proceeds appropriated to the North...the South, as the great exporting portion of the Union, has in reality paid vastly more than her due proportion of the revenue."

Lincoln's unfair bias for the North was obvious. He supported the more than tripling of the tariff percentage on goods coming into the southern ports which unfairly hurt the South. And he also was a proponent of what we now call "corporate welfare" for favored northern companies. In order to support his agenda, during the Civil War Abraham Lincoln effectively became a dictator, illegally ignoring the Constitution. He declared martial law and suspended the writ of Habeas Corpus. He imprisoned, without a trial, thousands of northern antiwar protesters even including the arrests of the mayor of Baltimore, its chief of police, a Maryland congressman and 31 state legislators. He shut down over 300 newspapers that disagreed with his war policy. He blockaded southern ports and invaded the South with troops without the consent of Congress as required by the Constitution. Lincoln also introduced taxation on income, which by the way is a mild form of slavery because you are forced to work a portion of each workday without getting paid. This has created an oppressive internal revenue bureaucracy that through the years has grown monstrously large.

Yes, Abraham Lincoln saved the Union but unfortunately the result was a giant blow to Liberty and effectively the death of "States Rights". The Federal Government was now much more powerful and tyrannical. The precedent had been set. Our great Constitution was now eroding away with greater centralized government power and a growing "police state" to protect that power.

This trend has slowly continued to this day where we no longer have a "government of the people, by the people and for the people". The American people need to demand proper representation in their government, a smaller constitutional Federal government and more freedom in their lives. Our founding fathers would no doubt be greatly disappointed if they had witnessed this growing apathy of the citizens through the years. I am hopeful that the light of Liberty will shine brightly once again here in the great United States of America.

Mark Flinchpaugh

Additional Publications by
J L Flinchpaugh Publishing Company
St. Joseph, Missouri

lflinch@stjoelive.com
www.larryflinchpaugh.com

John Larry Flinchpaugh Autobiography *Revised Edition October 2010. One copy each at St., Joseph, Mo Genealogy Library, Kirksville, Mo. City Library and the Cincinnati, Ohio Public Library.*

Secrets of Our Hidden Controllers Revealed, *November 1, 2009. Discover how the unelected controllers of our government control our lives and dictate what we do and think.*

Billions For The Bankers-Debts For The People, June 2009. *This 1984 informative 37 page reprint of Sheldon Emry's booklet will give the reader greater insight into our countries monetary system and explains why we must abolish the private Federal Reserve Banking cartel that has, from 1913, been in charge of printing our money and loaning it to the American government with interest. The U.S. Treasury Department should print our money "Interest Free."*

Growing Up In a Zoo, February 2011 *The story of Larry Flinchpaugh growing up in St. Joseph, Missouri in the 1940's through the 1960's and working in his parents Pet Shop, Zoo, and Reptile Gardens.*

Letters Home From Civil War Soldier Charles W. Gamble (1862-1864) *compiled by Mark Flinchpaugh, April 2011.*

Movie Documentary "This Is Our Town, St. Joseph, Missouri" *Filmed c. 1954*